Performance
and
Community

Performance and Community

Commentary and Case Studies

Edited by
Caoimhe McAvinchey

B L O O M S B U R Y

LONDON • NEW DELHI • NEW YORK • SYDNEY

Bloomsbury Methuen Drama

An imprint of Bloomsbury Publishing Plc

50 Bedford Square	1385 Broadway
London	New York
WC1B 3DP	NY 10018
UK	USA

www.bloomsbury.com

Bloomsbury is a registered trade mark of Bloomsbury Publishing Plc

British Library Cataloguing-in-Publication Data
A catalogue record for this book is available from the British Library.

ISBN: PB: 978-1-4081-4642-2
ePub: 978-1-4081-4726-9
ePDF:978-1-4081-4725-2

Library of Congress Cataloging-in-Publication Data
A catalog record for this book is available from the Library of Congress.

Typeset by Fakenham Prepress Solutions, Fakenham, Norfolk NR21 8NN
Printed and bound in India

For Cora and Paul McAvinchey

CONTENTS

CONTRIBUTORS

Ali Campbell has worked in the fields of educational, community and development theatre for 25 years. He is Senior Lecturer in Applied Performance at Queen Mary, University of London. Ali is one of the leading exponents and adaptors of the techniques of his teacher and mentor, the late Augusto Boal, the legendary Brazilian founder of the Theatre of the Oppressed movement.

Lily Einhorn works in participatory theatre, currently running the Two Boroughs Project at the Young Vic theatre. She has extensive experience in domestic violence prevention using drama, running the DV Schools Prevention Programme in Westminster. Lily has worked in a variety of contexts in both the UK and Paris with a diversity of groups. She has directed plays on the Edinburgh and London fringes and was assistant director for the Liverpool Capital of Culture opening ceremony.

Richard Ings is a writer and a researcher. Having taken Chinese Studies at Cambridge, where he wrote a dissertation on the revolutionary novelist Ding Ling, he has pursued a career first in publishing and then in the arts. For the last twenty years, he has published on a wide variety of cultural topics, from arts and health to venue pricing strategies, but has focused primarily on how the arts can contribute to positive social outcomes. Since obtaining a PhD in American Studies at Nottingham University, he has taught and published on visual culture and American photography, taking a special interest in the photographic representation of African American life.

Sue Mayo is a freelance theatre practitioner who has worked in a wide range of settings for more than thirty years. Sue specialises in devising theatre with community groups and frequently works across art forms, in collaboration with others. Sue is Associate Artist with Magic Me, an arts organisation specialising in bringing young and older people together through the arts. She is the author of *Detail & Daring: The Art and Craft of Intergenerational Work* (2012) and co-author, with Susan Langford, of *Sharing the Experience*, a handbook on intergenerational arts projects (2001). Sue is currently convenor of the MA in Applied Theatre at Goldsmiths, University of London.

Caoimhe McAvinchey is a Senior Lecturer in Drama, Theatre and Performance Studies at Queen Mary, University of London. Her research interests include socially engaged performance practices, documentation and the politics and practices of evaluation. Her recent book *Theatre & Prison* (2011) analyses the ways in which theatre makers have staged critical questions about the role of prison in society, the economy of punishment and the representation of criminal bodies. She is currently working on a research project about women, prison and performance.

Louise Owen works as a Lecturer in Theatre and Performance at Birkbeck, University of London. Her research examines contemporary theatre and performance in terms of economic change and modes of governance. Her recent publications explore site-specific performance, forms of immersive art and theatre, and performance and post-feminism. She is currently preparing a monograph about performance and neoliberalisation in Britain.

Martin Welton is Senior Lecturer in Theatre and Performance at Queen Mary, University of London. His research centres round the two broad thematic concerns of movement and the senses in relation to the theory and practice of contemporary performance. His most recent publications include essays on blackouts and darkness in the theatre, listening and attention in Rosemary Lee's *Common Dance*, and a monograph, *Feeling Theatre* (2011).

ACKNOWLEDGEMENTS

I would to thank Anna Brewer, Commissioning Editor at Bloomsbury Methuen Drama, for her vision in initiating this book and her patience and care in the realisation of the project. It has been a pleasure and privilege to imagine a book about theatre and performance practices that celebrates, challenges and reconfigures the relationship between performance and community.

I would like to thank all of the contributors – Ali Campbell, Lily Einhorn, Richard Ings, Sue Mayo, Louise Owen and Martin Welton – who have worked closely with artists and organisations to attend to aspects of their practice with insight and care. All of the individuals and companies featured in the book have been extraordinarily generous in their engagement with this project. In particular I would like to thank Jeremy Weller at Grassmarket Project, Sue Emmas and David Lan at the Young Vic, Jonathan Petherbridge at London Bubble, Susan Langford and Clea House at Magic Me and Geraldine Ling at Lawnmowers. Mark Storor and Anna Ledgard, Bobby Baker, Tony Fegan, Rosemary Lee, Mojisola Adebayo, Paul Heritage and Lois Weaver – thank you.

My wonderful colleagues and friends in Drama at Queen Mary, University of London have helped shape and inform this book through invigorating and sustaining conversations. The number of collaborators in this project – both contributors and subjects – who are connected with the department is testament to the rigorous, challenging and supportive environment we share. In particular, I would like to thank Jen Harvie and Michael McKinnie for making time and support available in the final stages of the manuscript preparation.

As ever, behind the scenes, there are people who through their small, daily acts of kindness make things possible:

Molly and Finn McFetridge arrived in the middle of this project bringing great joy and focus as well as sleeplessness; David McFetridge, for being your wonderful, generous and thoughtful self – thank you; Paul and Cora McAvinchey – for being wonderful parents and grandparents: this book is dedicated to you both, with love.

Introduction:
Right here, right now

Caoimhe McAvinchey

Performance and Community brings together artists, companies and creative producers whose work provokes a reconsideration of the relationship between ideas of performance and ideas of community. Rooted in the fields of applied, social and community performance, it speaks beyond sub-disciplinary boundaries to issues in the wider field of contemporary performance practice. The title, *Performance and Community*, declares the equal importance of both terms.

Two research questions frame the enquiry staged within the book. Firstly, what can performance practices, made in and with communities, reveal about the possibilities of performance as political and social practice? And, secondly, how do these practices critique and reimagine the idea of community perpetuated in contemporary political discourse – a magical place bound up in notions of safety, nostalgia or utopia?

In thinking about performance and community, there are many possible ways to identify or frame this work. We could think about community as being *where* the work takes place. This could be within a geographically defined area, as broadly considered as a region or as narrowly prescriptive as a housing estate or street. For example, the playwright Anne Jellicoe pioneered the Community Play, a model of making theatre in, with and for a specific community over a substantial period of time based on her experience of making *The Reckoning* (1978) in Lyme Regis.[1] Welfare State International (1968–2006), a collective of artists, developed new social processes that recognised and celebrated the daily lives and stories of communities. Their work ranged from large-scale spectacular events such as *Raising the Titanic* (London International Festival of Theatre [LIFT], 1983), a socialist critique of the development of London's docklands, through to more intimate explorations of new secular ceremonies for births and deaths.[2] Strange Cargo, a participatory arts organisation, based in Folkstone, specialises in large-scale participatory public art events in the local area. Projects such as *Cheriton Lights* (2013) – which culminated in a festival with fire sculptures, projections and art works with light – explicitly engaged with ideas of public space, community identity and cultural participation.[3]

The term 'communities of location' could also stretch to include more specific, institutional sites, such as schools, prisons, hospitals or residential care homes. There are many companies across the UK that specialise in working in specific institutional contexts, such as Geese Theatre (prisons), Ladder

---

[1]The Community Play has a number of practical frameworks and principles: a playwright works with a community research team to identify a theme that is of relevance and interest to a specific locality; there are large casts, over 100 people, with many more contributing to the production through, for example, fundraising, set building, costume making and marketing. Anne Jellicoe set up the Colway Theatre Trust in 1978 to explore and promote the Community Plays. Now called Claque Theatre (www.claquetheatre.com), the organisation continues to support communities in the UK, North America and Europe in the development and production of their own plays. Anne Jellicoe, *Community Plays: How to Put Them On* (London: Methuen, 1987) is a practical guide to developing both the infrastructural and creative frameworks for community collaboration.

[2]Baz Kershaw and Tony Coult, *Engineers of the Imagination: Welfare State International* (London: Methuen, 1990) offers both a critical introduction to their work as well as a practical guide to developing large-scale participatory practices. The *Dead Good Guides* invite readers to design and produce events that have significance for communities. See www.welfare-state.org.

[3]Strange Cargo, www.strangecargo.org.uk (accessed 27 February 2013).

to the Moon (dementia care settings) and Theatre Centre (schools). Whilst it may be easy to categorise people who happen to be in the same place at the same time under an umbrella identity, practitioners working in these contexts need to be mindful of whether or not the people living, working or attending these institutions recognise them as communities, or if they wish to be identified in relation to it.

People may choose to identify and gather themselves based on an aspect of their identity, such as age, gender, race, disability, sexuality, faith or ethnicity. If we adjust the frame of performance and community to include 'communities of interest' or 'communities of identity', a wide range of fluid, nuanced and responsive social processes is revealed.

The commitment of artists and theatre companies to work within community contexts – whether they are communities of location, interest and/identity – is not a recent phenomenon. These practices have their roots in the educational, alternative, radical and political theatre that flourished in the 1960s and 1970s: it is imperative that any examination of contemporary performances in and with communities is understood in this context.

In the UK, in the 1970s and 1980s, the alternative theatre movement fostered a flourishing of companies whose work was informed by identity politics, including Black Theatre Co-operative, British Asian Theatre, British Theatre of the Deaf, Siren Theatre Company, Beryl and the Perils and Half Moon Young People's Theatre.[4] Although some of these companies, such as Talawa, Red Ladder and Graeae, still operate, staging professional productions in tandem with their participatory work, many others, including the influential

---

[4]Unfinished Histories is a web-based project, directed by Susan Croft, documenting the British Alternative Movement (1968–88) through interviews and archive materials. It is an invaluable resource evidencing the political momentum and artistic invention that characterised some of the first Black, Asian, lesbian, gay, women's, disabled, theatre in education and community-based theatre groups in Britain.

Gay Sweatshop, Monstrous Regiment and 7:84, struggled to survive.[5]

The late 1990s and early 2000s witnessed a major shift in the economic, political and social values given to the arts in community contexts. In 1997 the Labour party came to government for the first time in nearly twenty years, promising to lead with 'strong values, the values of justice and progress and community'.[6] Central to this was a commitment to tackling social exclusion, a term defined by the government as, 'A shorthand label for what can happen when individuals or areas suffer from a combination of linked problems such as unemployment, poor skills, low incomes, poor housing, high crime environments, bad health and family breakdown'.[7] The Social Exclusion Unit worked across government departments, attempting to coordinate learning and policies within ministries to provide a coherent and ambitious strategy supporting individuals and communities throughout the country. The positive findings of Policy Action Team 10 (PAT 10), which examined the contribution of the sports and arts to neighbourhood renewal,[8] resonated with François Matarasso's *Use*

---

[5]For more information about community theatre in the context of the alternative movement see Sandy Craig (ed.), *Dreams and Deconstructions: Alternative Theatre in Britain* (Ambergate: Amber Lane Press Ltd, 1980) and Maria Di Cenzo, *The Politics of alternative theatre in Britain 1968–90: The Case of 7:84 (Scotland)* (Cambridge: Cambridge University Press, 1996). The work of specific companies is documented in John McGrath, *A Good Night Out* (London: Methuen, 1981); Philip Osment, *Gay Sweatshop: Four Plays and a Company* (London: Methuen, 1989) and Gillian Hanna (ed.), *Monstrous Regiment: Four Plays and a Collective Celebration* (London: Nick Hern Books, 1991).

[6]Tony Blair, general election victory speech, 1997. British Political Speech Archive, http://www.britishpoliticalspeech.org/speech-archive.htm?speech=222 (accessed 2 January 2013).

[7]Social Exclusion Unit, *Social Exclusion Unit: Purpose, Work Priorities and Working Methods* (London: The Stationery Office, 1997).

[8]See PAT 10, 'National Strategy for Neighbourhood Renewal. Policy Action Team Audit. Report of the Policy Action Team 10: The Contribution of Sports and the Arts' (London: DCMS, 1999).

or Ornament? The Social Impact of Participation in the Arts (1997). In his report, Matarasso identified fifty discreet benefits of participation in the arts, urging a recalibration of attitude and investment to the arts in community contexts in order 'to start talking about what the arts can do for society, rather than what society can do for the arts'.[9] Although Matarasso has since received substantial criticism – both about the methodological framework for the research and the implications it has had for cultural policy and practice – it was, at the time of publication, a persuasive factor in New Labour's 70 per cent increased investment in the arts: much of this resource was directed towards practices that explicitly set out to ameliorate the pathways to, and effects of, social exclusion.[10]

The impact of this investment in the arts as a means of driving social *inclusion* was evidenced in the late 1990s and throughout the 2000s, when participatory performance work with groups or communities categorised by a specific issue, or aspect of identity, mushroomed: young people in pupil referral units, refugees, isolated elders and the homeless suddenly had an abundance of opportunity to participate in arts programmes; arts organisations had new funding possibilities available to them; freelance arts practitioners had a wealth of employment opportunities; and new university courses in

---

[9] François Matarasso, *Use or Ornament? The Social Impact of Participation in the Arts* (Stroud: Comedia, 1997), p. iv.
[10] Both Paola Merli, 'Evaluating the Social Impact of Participation in Arts Activities: A Critical Review of François Matarasso's *Use or Ornament?*' in *International Journal of Cultural Policy*, vol. 8, no. 1 (2002), pp. 107–18 and Eleonora Belfiore and Oliver Bennett, *The Social Impact of the Arts: An Intellectual History* (Basingstoke: Palgrave Macmillan, 2010) provide a rigorous critique of Matarasso's work. Arts Council England reports by Helen Jermyn, *The Arts and Social Exclusion: A Review Prepared for the Arts Council of England* (London: ACE, 2001) and *The Arts of Inclusion* (London: ACE, 2004) give useful access to how government was thinking about the relationship between arts, participation and community engagement.

Applied Drama examined the cultural, social and political value of this work.

However, the economic and social opportunities for performance in community contexts afforded through these policies have also had delimiting impacts both on perceptions of it and the language used to discuss it. Performance practices categorising communities through their perceived risk or experience of social exclusion offer only a partial picture: individuals and groups identified as *being* something highlights only that aspect of themselves, i.e. prisoner, homeless, refugee, teenage parent. Such singularity of approach negates the glorious complexity of human beings and how fluid, accommodating or even contradictory our identities and notions of community can be. In additional to this, rather than discuss the political or aesthetic ambitions for work, cultural workers were expected to confidently articulate a particular promise: that their work would have a positive social impact. Furthermore, it was also understood that the promised impact would be accounted for within a financial linguistic framework – providing funders with proof of the social return on their investment in the arts.[11]

James Thompson's *Performance Affects: Applied Theatre and the End of Effect* critiques the impact of the language of effect and value within applied performance practices whilst proposing new models of theoretical engagement that reframe its political, aesthetic and affective possibilities.[12] Recent work by Helen Nicholson, Anthony Jackson, Joe Winston and Nicola Shaughnessy has extended academic discourse about performance in educational, community and social contexts to examine ideas of beauty, play, empathy

---

[11] New Philanthropy Capital's report *Unlocking Value: The Economic Value of the Arts in Criminal Justice* (London: New Philanthropy Capital, 2011) is a useful illustration of the difficulty in accounting for the social return on investment, particularly in contexts where people are considered to be 'at risk' of social exclusion.

[12] James Thompson, *Performance Affects: Applied Theatre and the End of Effect* (Basingstoke: Palgrave Macmillan, 2009).

and embodiment.[13] In the fields of Visual Culture and Contemporary Performance two significant contributions have invigorated ideas about participatory performance practices. Claire Bishop's *Artificial Hells: Participatory Art and the Politics of Spectatorship* counters and critiques assumptions that participation in socially engaged arts practices promotes emancipatory social relations whilst Shannon Jackson's *Social Works: Performing Arts, Supporting Publics* argues that all performance is social work and that there is a mutually dependent relationship between art and publics.[14]

Performance and Community contributes to these debates by foregrounding the voices and practices of artists and organisations committed to working in community contexts. Together they have forged new possibilities for who makes performance, where it takes place, the terrains it negotiates and the artistic forms it engages.

The work of Magic Me, The Lawnmowers, the Grassmarket Project, London Bubble and the partnership between artist Mark Storor and producer Anna Ledgard is examined through a series of case studies. These provide an historical overview of each company or partnership and, by focusing on particular projects or performances, give access to the politics of these practices. Interviews with Lois Weaver, Mojisola Adebayo, Bobby Baker, Rosemary Lee, Sue Emmas, Tony Fegan and Paul Heritage evidence the complexity and ambition of work committed to negotiating a delicate partnership with people

---

[13] Anthony Jackson, *Theatre, Education and the Making of Meaning* (Manchester: Manchester University Press, 2007); Helen Nicholson, *Theatre, Education and Performance* (Basingstoke: Palgrave, 2011); Nicola Shaughnessy, *Applying Performance: Live Art, Socially Engaged Theatre and Affective Practice* (Basingstoke: Palgrave Macmillan, 2011); Jo Winston, *Beauty and Education* (London: Routledge, 2010).

[14] Claire Bishop, *Artificial Hells: Participatory Art and the Politics of Spectatorship* (London: Verso, 2012). Shannon Jackson, *Social Works: Performing Art, Supporting Publics* (London: Routledge, 2011).

gathering as communities of curiosity, to explore and make performance together.

The wide and provocative range of performance practices within the collection are characterised by dimensionality. This work is complex, nuanced, rigorous and both politically and aesthetically ambitious for the possibilities of what is possible when people work together through performance.

Performance in community and social contexts often has limited accessibility to a general public audience. Although many contemporary companies have websites that illustrate aspects of the work they do, there is a substantial gap between a brief description of a project on a webpage and a detailed engagement and reflection on it. *Performance and Community* gives unprecedented access into the working practices of artists, creative producers and companies pioneering work in community and social contexts. The decision to alternate case studies and interviews allows for connections and resonances between different performance practices and to illuminate points of connection rather than distinctions between them.

Whilst many of the individuals and organisations featured in the collection are based in London, the reach and impact of their work – through touring, teaching and networks of collaboration – is national and international. This work may be specifically located in response to a particular group – for example, critically ill children, their families and the hospital staff who care for them – but the principles of each approach informs an entire body of practice.

A number of the contributors or subjects within the book have connections with Drama at Queen Mary, University of London. This was not an explicit intention for the project, but emerged through its development, reflecting the diverse, accommodating and dialogic research environment that the department fosters.

The case studies and interviews

Lois Weaver's work reclaims and re-evaluates the excluded and ignored. Since the 1970s, her work as a performer, director, activist and teacher has been driven by a feminist imperative to investigate both the everyday (such as laundry) and the institutional (such as the museum, the library and the archive) and to theatricalise them so that they speak of the things that aren't usually valued within them. Her collaborations with Spiderwoman, Split Britches, Bloolips and Holly Hughes have toured globally to popular and critical acclaim. This work, along with the formation of the WOW Café – a performance space run by women for women in New York's Lower East Side – has informed major critical contributions about lesbian performance, feminist performance and butch/femme aesthetics within Performances Studies.[15]

Weaver's work in community and social contexts runs in parallel to and in conversation with the development of her performance work. Projects such as AGLOW (Association of Greater London Older Women), *Staging Human Rights*[16] with women in prison and *Democratising Technology*, a research project that uses performance techniques to initiate conversations on technology design, have received less academic consideration than her solo or collaborative performance

---

[15] Elaine Aston and Sue-Ellen Case (eds), *Staging International Feminisms* (Basingstoke: Palgrave Macmillan, 2007); Lizbeth Goodman, *The Routledge Reader in Gender and Performance* (London and New York: Routledge, 1998); Sue Ellen Case (ed.), *Split Britches: Lesbian Practice/Feminist Performance* (London and New York: Routledge, 1996); Alisa Solomon, 'The WOW Café', *Drama Review* 29, no. 1 (1985), pp. 92–101.

[16] Lois Weaver, 'Doing Time: A Personal and Practical Account of Making Performance Work in Prisons' in Tim Prentki and Shelia Preston (eds), *The Applied Theatre Reader* (London and New York: Routledge, 2008), pp. 81–94; Caoimhe McAvinchey, 'Unexpected Acts: Women, Prison and Performance" in Michael Balfour and John Sommers (eds.), *Drama as Social Intervention* (Concord, Ontario: Captus University Press, 2006), pp. 216–27.

work. Underpinned by an activist agenda informed by practical feminism and social justice, Weaver's grassroots practice offers a unique contribution to reconsider the possibilities of performance as a strategy for community capacity building. In this interview Weaver reflects on recent developments in her work, particularly Public Address Systems, a series of performance structures that invite people to meet, talk and, through this collaboration, both understand and undertake the political work that needs to be done in their specific context. For Weaver, the practical politics of community are embodied in the idea of a coalition of people with a particular job to do at a particular moment in time.

Sue Mayo's case study of **Magic Me,** an intergenerational arts organisation based in the London borough of Tower Hamlets, reveals the diversity of communities identifying themselves through ethnicity or faith in one of the most socially and economically deprived boroughs in the UK. Here, the arts are engaged to facilitate community development in a place where people are isolated. This isolation is not just *between* ethnically identified communities but also *within* these communities. Mayo examines two Magic Me projects, *The Wisdom of all Ages* and *Stepping Out in Stepney*, that brought together participants across four generations, an act that she proposed created 'temporary community'. Mayo argues that this idea of community is valuable precisely because its temporality encourages individuals to experiment with those 'who look and sound different, who move differently, who have different histories'.

Mojisola Adebayo is a writer, performer and director whose work, fuelled by a critical examination of the politics of race, gender and sexuality, stages the negotiation of personal and political identities.[17] For Adebayo, thinking

---

[17]Mojisola Adebayo, *Plays 1: Moj of the Antarctic, Muhammad Ali and Me, Desert Boy & Matt Henson, North Star* (Ottawa: Oberon Books, 2011); Mojisola Adebayo, '48 Minutes for Palestine' in Anna Furse (ed.), *Theatre in*

about performance and 'communities of interest' allows for a consideration of the needs and desires that draw people together. In her interview she reflects on the development of *I Stand Corrected*, her most recent play, examining the culture of violence that, she argues, condones the so-called corrective rape of lesbians in South Africa and (at the time of interview) the British state's resistance to facilitating gay marriage. During the devising process, Adebayo worked with black lesbians from townships around Cape Town to explore these issues and their voices are, literally, present within the work, travelling across time and cultures to participate in a wider political debate about race, gender and sexuality.

Adebayo has extensive experience of working in international contexts, often where performance is called upon to negotiate between communities fractured by war or with groups of people on the edge of mainstream society. She is currently a mentor for Shout!, a new arts collective supporting black, Asian, minority, ethnic, refugee, lesbian, gay, bi-sexual, transgender, queer, inter-sex young people based in Ovalhouse, London. This, like all of Adebayo's work, realises an activist impulse that demands a space, through performance, for 'the minority in the minority'.

Adebayo, Mayo and Weaver each articulate the personal commitments that people make to be together through performance, for a particular moment in time with a specific job to do. Whilst recognising the long-term potential impacts of participation in a shared collaborative practice, they remind us not to ignore the political potential and value of the temporary community, of negotiated togetherness, right here, right now.

The Lawnmowers Independent Theatre Company is a ground-breaking company led by learning disabled adults. Ali Campbell's case study gives insight into over twenty years of work made by, for and with learning disabled adults. Since its formation in 1986, the Lawnmowers have had a profound

---

Pieces: Politics, Poetics and Interdisciplinary Collaboration – An Anthology of Play Texts from 1968–2010 (London: Methuen, 2011).

impact on the lives of thousands of learning-disabled adults, their families and carers. It has also, through developing national and international partnership networks with local government, universities and trade unions, provoked a considerable reassessment and understanding of learning disabled adults' experience, expertise and ability. The Lawnmowers' practice is informed by the approaches of Augusto Boal and Dorothy Heathcote, positioning the participant as author and agent who, through reflexive awareness, becomes adept in, 'distilling personal experience into political expertise'. By asking a series of questions about pedagogy, community-making and belonging, Campbell calls upon specific moments of performance across two decades, illuminating the politics of the Lawnmowers practice. Through this case study we see the Lawnmowers as a company, a place (Swinbourne House in Newcastle) and an approach informed by the concept of *philoxenia*, a Greek term for hospitality that welcomes the guest as a gift to be celebrated. This sense of being recognised, of being valued for who you are, permeates the Lawnmowers' practice and has strong resonances in the work that Bobby Baker discusses in her interview.

Bobby Baker is a performance artist who, over the past four decades, has made work characterised by sharp social commentary, humour and the unexpected – meringue ladies, frozen peas and ladle dancing have all featured in her performances, which have gained considerable popular and critical success internationally.[18] Baker's inclusion in a collection investigating performance and community may be a surprise for people more familiar with works such as *How To Live* (2007), a show staged in major cultural institutions playing to audiences of thousands each night or programmed as part of international festivals of theatre. However, throughout her career, Baker has been committed to staging her work in

---

[18] Michele Barrett and Bobby Baker (eds), *Bobby Baker: Redeeming Features of Everyday Life* (London and New York: Routledge, 2007).

places where people meet rather than to places where theatre audiences go: women's refuges, day centres and village halls. Her work offers an invitation to audiences to consider her 'passionate concerns' – family, the value of domestic work and the language used to discuss mental illness.

In this interview, Baker talks about the work she has been developing with her company, Daily Life Limited, particularly *Mad Gyms and Kitchens* and *The Daily Life Project*, fuelled by a political necessity to create spaces – both real and virtual – for people who, like Baker, have also had experience of mental illness and recovery, to share their top tips for wellness: their small, daily acts of survival. Both projects are characterised by a generosity of spirit and a political commitment to tackling the stigma and discrimination experienced by people with mental illness, creating networks of knowledge, capacity and resilience.[19]

Richard Ings' case study of the **Grassmarket Project** examines Jeremy Weller's uncompromising approach to making theatre with and about people on the margins of mainstream society. The language of government policy – of 'social inclusion', of 'young people at risk of social exclusion' – that shaped so much of the arts funding agenda in the 2000s is revealed as being entirely incapable of describing or containing the chaotic intensity of the lives they allude to. The terms of many of these funding streams expected artists and arts organisations working in participatory contexts to identify and prescribe particular social benefits for both individuals and society as a causal result of people's engagement in their projects. Weller's work exposes both the fragility and dishonesty of this proposition and reminds us – artists, scholars and audiences – to interrogate the discourses that shape the cultural and economic contexts that facilitate the production of work that explicitly address social exclusion.

---

[19] Bobby Baker, *Diary Drawings: Mental Illness and Me* (London: Profile Books, 2010).

Focusing on the production of *The Foolish Young Man*, Ings mirrors Weller's invitation to the audience, inviting us to engage with the horrific realities of a world where some young people are pushed to the edges of society through their experiences of drugs, gangs and violence. Weller's project is a commitment to the theatre as a 'laboratory in which all humanity can be explored'. He demands that audiences interrogate both nostalgic or utopian ideas of community and their own position in challenging or maintaining a status quo that supports grievous social inequity. His work calls for us to attend to 'the other' living alongside us.

This call to attend, to pay attention and care for others also frames and permeates the work of choreographer **Rosemary Lee**. Lee's work extends across a spectrum of platforms, from dances-for-camera through to choreographic practices working with large casts of non-professional dancers. In this interview, Martin Welton highlights Lee's desire to work beyond definitions of identity that may limit how people see themselves and each other to find ways of being together and recognising what is shared rather than different. Focusing on the performance *Common Dance*, Lee reflects on the robust choreographic structures that offer a spaciousness for people to be together, to care for each other, witnessed by an audience. Lee's work models a politics of collaboration, an ethic of care, of responsibility for oneself and each other, that reaches beyond the rehearsal room and performance space and into the world.

In her case study of **London Bubble**, Louise Owen details the development of the theatre company from its inception in 1972 as a local government initiative to bring theatre to the people of London. The study outlines the major socio-political and economic factors that impacted upon the company's artistic and operational practices, ultimately shaping the company's current identity as an organisation committed to participatory arts practice within its locality. Focusing on two interlinked projects, *Grandchildren of the Blitz and Blackbirds*, Owen examines how these projects prompted participants to reconsider their sense of time, place and history within a local community context. The case study gives extraordinary access to the complex layers of participation that informed and shaped both the research and devising process to create a performance that was in, with and very much about the community that made it.

London's **Young Vic Theatre** has an international reputation for developing new work and mentoring young theatre makers, particularly directors. It is an off-West End venue that prides itself on its commitment to making theatre available to the residents of its home boroughs of Lambeth and Southwark, whilst engaging with an international audience: 'With roots deep in our neighbourhoods, we reach out to theatre makers across the globe.'[20] Lily Einhorn's interview with Sue Emmas, the founder and director of Taking Part, the Young Vic's participatory programmes department, details the theatre's commitment to its local, diverse community and the interweaving strands of opportunity that facilitate residents' access to the building, its productions and theatre-making processes. The Young Vic is the only building-based theatre organisation represented in the collection and Emmas's reflections facilitate a deeper under-standing of the cultural, social and educational opportunities that a physical site and organisational structures afford to the theatre in its continuing offer of invitation to its local community.

Sue Mayo's case study of the partnership between the artist **Mark Storor** and the producer **Anna Ledgard** examines the negotiated structures that enable a genuine collaboration between the artist and participants. She examines the expectations and demands made of artists working in community contexts, particularly the political and ethical implications of authorship and ownership in collective creative labour. She examines *For the Best*, a project, performance and installation

---

[20] Ruth Little, *The Young Vic Book: Theatre Work and Play* (London: Methuen, 2004); Young Vic website, http://www.youngvic.org/about-us (accessed 27th February 2013).

devised in collaboration with children and adults with chronic renal disease in the Evelina Children's Hospital in London and the Royal Liverpool University Hospital. Months of detailed negotiation with the hospital staff enabled the creative work at patients' bedsides, working around their experience of everyday life with dialysis treatment. Mayo's case study details the practical politics of Storor's collaborative work, particularly the time that is needed to build understanding, relationships and the space to creatively explore ideas together.

Tony Fegan is a theatre director, creative producer, community activist and currently Director of Tallaght Community Arts (TCA) in Ireland. Fegan was the first Director of Learning for the London International Festival of Theatre (LIFT) (1993–2007) and his influence on contemporary participatory arts practices in the UK and beyond has been considerable. During his time at LIFT he pioneered large-scale international and inter-cultural learning programmes in community contexts. These programmes were central rather than peripheral to LIFT's activities, modelling a political commitment to participant-centred learning, critical investigation and aesthetic vision.[21] The legacy of this is considerable: international artists and companies coming to LIFT entered into a relationship with audiences, often in specific community contexts; arts organisations in London recognised the investment of time, skills and funding required to develop partnerships and commission community-based work of this scale and integrity; artists – including Mark Storor and Bobby Baker, who are also featured in this collection – were given practical and intellectual support to push the possibilities of what performance practice in communities could be.

---

[21] For more information about LIFT generally and the learning progamme specifically see Rose Fenton and Lucy Neal, *The Turning World: Stories from the London International Festival of Theatre* (London: Calouste Gulbenkian Foundation, 2005); Julia Rowntree, *Changing the Performance: A Companion Guide to Arts, Business and Civic Engagement* (London and New York: Routledge, 2006); and LIFT Living Archive, http://www.liftlivingarchive.com/lla/ (accessed 1st March 2013).

In this interview Fegan discusses the work he has been developing as Director of Tallaght Community Arts (TCA), based in South Dublin, an area that has limited cultural infrastructure and, in post Celtic-Tiger Ireland, even less financial resource. His reflections reveal many things about the nature of leading a small arts organisation committed to being of service to its local community. TCA acts as a connecting and capacity building resource; it facilitates dialogue within the local community, between local residents and their governmental representatives whilst also actively countering a national prejudice that Tallaght is a dystopian world.

Paul Heritage is an academic, theatre director, creative producer and cultural ambassador whose work, for over three decades, has been characterised by its commitment to social justice through international and intercultural exchange. Heritage has developed organisational structures, within a university context, to facilitate interdisciplinary dialogue and collaborations with a range of partners: from prisons and probation officers in the UK through to the Ministers for Justice and Culture in Brazil.[22] Within the UK, performance practice within the prison system or with young people who are considered to be at risk of (re)entering it has primarily been framed and valued on its ability to address offending behaviours and reduce recidivism. Heritage offers an important challenge to this, arguing that an individual operates within institutional and social structures: unless the institutional hierarchies recognise this, work with individuals can only hope to have a limited impact. His large-scale, multi-partner projects develop local, national and international networks committed to social change.

Artists working in community contexts have to negotiate perceptions and expectations of authenticity, agency and

---

[22] Heritage established the Theatre in Prisons and Probation Centre at Manchester University with James Thompson in 1992 and People's Palace Project, an applied performance research unit and arts organisation at QMUL in 1999.

authority, and in this interview Heritage recognises the critical reflexivity that the position of being an outsider to a particular group or community affords him: he is an English academic who frequently works in the *favelas* of Rio de Janeiro. He invites us to consider how, time and again, artists take responsibility to critique the actions of the state, particularly regarding issues of punishment, and when it is either absent or ineffectual. Ultimately, Heritage asks, What can we do? What should we do?

The artists, companies and creative producers featured in this book have responded to this call to action, evidencing why and how performance can be a politically and aesthetically ambitious critical engagement with the world.

Conclusion

Performance and Community is a provocation to reimagine the necessity of performance in, with, by, for and about communities. The dialogues within the book invite us not only to consider the political work that performance is engaged in in various community contexts and the innovative forms it engenders but also to examine and be more demanding of the possibilities *for* community.

The multiplicity of meanings of, and desires for, 'community' reveal it as a term and social process that is fluid and complex. Raymond Williams' approach to community from a cultural materialist approach accommodates some of this ambiguity when he writes: 'Community can be the warmly persuasive word to describe an existing set of relationships, or the warmly persuasive word to describe an alternative set of relationships.'[23] The word can have connotations of unity, consensus and sameness. But community is also a highly charged word and idea: as a form of social organisation, it

---

[23] Raymond Williams, *Keywords: A Vocabulary of Culture and Society* (New York: Oxford University Press, 1983), p. 76

simultaneously prompts a sense of belonging and exclusion. You are either one of us or one of them. In post-industrial Britain, community is a slippery term that rejects precise definition. Often it's easier to describe what it *isn't*. In the wake of the riots across and beyond London in the summer of 2011, the word community was usually evoked with a sense of yearning for a way that the world had once been: an idealised state of all being well with the world, a welcoming place somewhere along the road between nostalgia and utopia.

Sociologists including Zygmunt Bauman and Gerard Delanty, political scientist Benedict Anderson, philosopher Giorgio Agamben and cultural theorist Miranda Joseph have interrogated ideas and expectations infused within the word 'community', providing an invaluable reassessment of its relationship with ideas of modernity, nationalism, capitalism and globalisation.[24] Within the context of a globalised world, where neo-liberalism further cleaves the gap of social inequity between the richest and poorest people, each of the artists, companies and creative producers featured in *Performance and Community* contribute directly to this discourse. Their performance-based approaches invite people to join them in thinking about the world; to participate and collaborate in negotiating new pathways of understanding through the terrains of race, sexuality, faith, health and wellbeing, community development, learning disabled advocacy, freedom of expression, the local and the international. This collection of case studies and interviews offers an opportunity to think not just about *what* they make but *how* they make it and why this matters. The collection evidences how this ethical and

---

[24] Zygmunt Bauman, *Community: Seeking Safety in an Insecure World* (Oxford: Polity, 2000); Gerard Delanty, *Community: Key Ideas* (London: Routledge, 2003); Giorgio Agamben, *The Coming Community* (Minneapolis: University of Minnesota Press, 1993); Benedict Anderson, *Imagined Communities: Reflections on the Origin and Spread of Nationalism* (London: Verso 2006); Miranda Joseph, *Against the Romance of Community* (Minneapolis: University of Minnesota Press, 2002).

political engagement in and with communities challenges and innovates contemporary performance-making practices.

These models of social practice help us to recognise each other as more than the issues or labels of community identity that are so easily put upon us. They invite us to attend to each other within a framework crafted through principles of intimacy, care, equity and justice. Ultimately, *Performance and Community* gives access to performance, in and with communities, as a site of negotiated togetherness that allows us to identify, articulate, and act upon shared concerns: to jump the ethical gap between the way things are and the way things could be.

1

Lois Weaver

Interview and introduction by Caoimhe McAvinchey

Lois Weaver is a performance artist, writer, director and activist. She is also Professor of Contemporary Performance at Queen Mary, University of London. She was co-founder of Spiderwoman Theatre, Split Britches Company and the WOW Cafe in New York and Artistic Director of Gay Sweatshop Theatre in London.

As a director, writer and performer, projects include *Miss America* (2008), *Lesbians Who Kill* (1992), *Belle Reprieve* with Bloolips (1991), *Little Women: The Tragedy* (1988), *Dress Suits for Hire* (1987) with Peggy Shaw and Holly Hughes and *Upwardly Mobile Home* (1984). Weaver's work is internationally recognised as a provocation for new ways of seeing and staging radical, lesbian, feminist bodies.

Her experiments in performance as a means of public engagement include the development of *The Long Table, The Library of Performing Rights, The FeMUSEum* and her facilitating persona, Tammy WhyNot.

She was a partner in *Staging Human Rights*, a People's Palace Project that employed performance practice to explore human rights in women's prisons in Brazil, and the UK director for *PSi#12: Performing Rights*, an international conference and festival on performance and human rights.

* * *

What performance projects are you involved in at the moment?

One of the things I'm trying to do right now is make sense of all the different things that I have done over the past four decades. I'm writing a book, trying to historicise my own process, looking at the turning points in which I became an artist, because I feel like every project offers me a way to be a different kind of artist. I'm looking at the kinds of materials that I've worked with – community, place and laundry – and put those materials into the same basket and said, What do these things do? One of the things I have tried to do is to address things through the study, use and subversion of different forms of performance.

In terms of onstage creative work, I'm working on an autobiographical piece called *Age Fright*, which parallels age fright and stage fright and is part of my larger research project looking at ageing, intimacy and fear.

I've also been working with Peggy Shaw on her show *Ruff*. We've always used performance to interrogate the personal stages of our development in our lives. In this particular stage, it was Peggy's experience of having had a stroke. So we're looking at the issues of memory when someone has had some loss of memory, we're also looking at how one responds to that extreme situation and where is the place of the imagination in the neuroscience of memory loss and structural damage. It was commissioned by PS122 and a theatre in Alaska called Out North and we've just finished doing that performance as a part of the COIL Festival in Dixon Place, New York. It's been an incredibly satisfying collaboration because it felt like it really brought together the thirty-three years of our having developed a language on how we use performance to address these larger issues, such as ageing, and incorporate personal detail into that investigation.

I'm also generating a website called *Public Address Systems* that looks at how performance engages the public around issues through re-appropriating or re-purposing the everyday: things like *The Long Table, The Library of Performing Rights or The FeMUSEum.*

What was The FeMUSEum?

The FeMUSEum was a commission by an AHRC funded initiative called *Performance Matters*, looking at the cultural value of performance. Within this, they ran a symposium – Trashing Performance. They approached me because of my trashy Tammy persona. Trash performance is primarily a gay male territory and I wanted to establish a female presence in it. One way of doing that was to create a kind of repository of feminine or femme, which is a hyper-feminine, materials. I invited Amy Lamé, Bird la Bird and Carmelita Tropicana to work with me and we each chose three femme muses, responded to them and created a performance installation called *The FeMUSEum.*

We took over the Court Room at Toynbee Studios and set that up as the museum. But it was actually empty, a panelled courtroom with white plinths and nothing on them. There was a big sign that said 'Exit to the Gift Shop'. Everything we made in response to the representations of the muses was in the gift shop. It was a big, crazy church bazaar kind of shop. Amy Lamé was running a tea shop where you had to calculate the price of tea based on how little money women make compared to men. Carmelita Tropicana was doing a response to Sor Juana, a seventeenth-century Mexican letter writer and lesbian nun, writing letters for people. I was Dolly Parton with a thrift store based on the femme things I inherited from my Aunt Edna, who was one of my muses. I was giving away bells because Ellen Stewart, the founder of La MaMa Experimental

FIGURE 1 *Carmelita Tropicana, Bird la Bird, Lois Weaver and Amy Lamé, The FeMUSEum (2011).*

Theater Club in New York, introduced performances by ringing a hand-bell, saying, 'Never underestimate the power of the bell.' Ellen Stewart also said that if you have your own push-cart, basically, you can accomplish anything, so I also handed out little cut-out carts with the prompt: make your own pushcart and see where it will take you.

Again, it was using things like libraries, museums, dinner tables – things that were mundane and institutional – and trying to theatricalise them so that they speak of things that don't normally get included in them. *The FeMUSEum* was about the lack of the feminine within the museum or within the repositories of culture. It was a response to institutional male dominated museums and it looked at women's work, the commodification of women's work and the place women often occupy in institutional spaces.

The Library of Performing Rights – *can you contextualise that a little bit more?*

The *Library of Performing Rights* came out of my directorship of *Performing Rights*, the Performance Studies International conference in 2006 that focussed on the intersection between performance and human rights. In thinking about how to programme performance alongside the conference, it became quite clear that a lot of performance work that engages with human rights is not really tourable or easily documented, or it's often a process-oriented performance work with people in remote areas. So we asked, how can we make that available to people through a virtual library where we could actually have virtual contact with people who are doing that work around the world?

We put out a call for donations for any materials from anybody who worked in what they thought would be the intersection of performance and human rights, or performance and social justice. We collected loads of materials – DVDs, books, pamphlets, posters – and we made a library art installation. It had a manifesto room, where people could come in and just perform their manifestos, which we also documented. As a result of that we ended up with a body of materials that we toured to Vienna and Glasgow, where we did a smaller version of the *Performing Rights Festival*. It's in the study room at the Live Art Development Agency so people have access to it. Now I'm working with Andrew Mitchelson to create satellite versions – there was an installation of the *Library of Performing Rights* at the Panorama Festival in Rio in November 2012, and at that point they did a call out for more materials. So those materials will stay in Brazil and then they're working to expand that to other cities in Latin and South America. So we are trying to create a more fluid idea of what the library is, rather than just a collection of books. It's a concept around which people can contribute and interact with materials and people who are doing this kind of work.

The Library of Performing Rights *is a structure and an invitation to people to talk and work together, just like* The Long Table ...

Yes. The thing I'm most interested in right now is inventing ways to get people to talk to each other – how to turn an audience that's forward facing into facing each other and having a conversation with each other and *The Long Table* is part of this.

It uses the dinner table setting as a means for encouraging public conversation. I bring the table into a public place and set it up as if it were a dinner table. I talk about what a dinner table is, the kinds of manners, behaviours and conversation we bring to the dinner table and consider how to overlay that with some serious topics.

There are some people who are invited to the table because of a particular interest in the topic that frames the discussion but there are always spaces at the table to allow people from the audience to come and go, to join in the conversation. I'm very careful to talk about *The Long Table* as being a *seeded* conversation because otherwise people do come to it with an expectation that they will *present* and that creates a different dynamic. It's hard to get people to understand that if they sit back and allow for silence and awkwardness, something will come – people will talk with each other.

The first *Long Table* was in Rio in 2003, as part of *In the House*, an installation about women in prison. Since then I've curated a *Long Table* on citizenship, a *Long Table* on the performance of violence within socially engaged practice, a *Long Table* on the idea of the changing body where we dealt with trans bodies or other kinds of bodies in transition, such as immigration.

With The Long Table *you've devised a structure with protocol to support conversation and it's out there, in circulation, being used by others. So is* Public Address Systems *both a series of approaches to public engagement through*

FIGURE 2 *Lois Weaver hosting* The Long Table.

performance and a website which holds information about them?

Yes. The website is my attempt at holding these things together and to disseminate them. So on the website there will be a takeaway, which is a PDF do-it-yourself kit for *The Long Table*, *Porch Sitting* and the *Card Table*, which is looking at how to break down a panel presentation.

Can you explain more about Porch Sitting?

What I've done for that is to take a theatre and invite people to come and sit in it, to look at an empty stage and just talk. The prompts to each other or to themselves are things like, 'When's the last time you saw ...?' Or, 'What is that just down the road?' Or, 'Whatever happened to ...?' The kinds of prompts that we might have if we were just sitting with people with no real agenda of having to have a conversation. Things I associate, certainly having grown up in the rural south of the United States, with sitting on the porch. It's about 'I wonder', it's not about 'I know' or 'I think'. There's an implicit question or an implicit rumination rather than a display of knowledge.

At a Split Britches anniversary at La MaMa in April 2012 we did a *Porch Sitting* for, as it turned out, the future of queer and feminist performance: it was a wonderful conversation. We had about sixty people, talking non-stop, about the current sense of diaspora that young artists feel, especially in New York, because of economics: there's no longer the East Village where people can just do their work; people are scattered all over. So we were asking questions like, How can we have a performance community? How can we pull this kind of performance community together like there was in the eighties when we're so spread out and we live two hours away? Where are the venues that will support us in the way that WOW did? Some really important things happened at that event. One of the producers from La MaMa and a young entrepreneurial gay performance artist got together and created a whole new series for young queer artists at La MaMa. So there were connections made and some really great outcomes from it, but it was just set up as a way to talk about what shall we do now? And I think that's the general undertone, what do we do now?

Why is it important to have conversations without an agenda?

Everything I've ever done comes down to my own fears and limitations – the kinds of performance work that I made, the way that I invented the methodologies for making my own work, the way I used my own personal material as subject matter for my work, or the way I use association and impulse as the bedrock for my work. This was all about the things that I felt like I didn't know how to do and therefore I invented a way to do them. I think these kinds of conversations and protocols for conversation come from the way that I feel when I sit in a public environment and have something to say but feel terrified to say it, or feel less than, or feel like that my experience or my expertise is not as important as someone who may be more knowledgeable.

It's also a way of me coming to terms with my own idea of what democracy is. And to me – and I think this has really dictated all of my work, all of my community building and performance building – has been everyone deserves a voice and everyone deserves a place at the table. That's the basis of my feminism: how can I make situations where we all have a place at the table where the anecdote, the personal story, the theoretical point and the statistical piece of data have a place – that one thing's not privileged over another. I was also thinking about safety, what it means to make a safe space. I don't tend to use that word very often because I think it's really complicated, but it's also true. Whenever I walk into that room, whether it's students or whether it's people who are engaged with technology for the first time at the age of eighty or whether it's women in prison, my goal is to make them feel safe enough to make something, do something, say something. The greatest compliment is when people come up to me after a performance and say, You made me feel like I could do that. And there is something about that kind of empowering through doing. This started happening with me when I started working with Spiderwoman, and I've pulled it through WOW and I've pulled it through Split Britches and now into the wider areas of teaching and organising.

Are you still involved with WOW – the Woman's One World Cafe?

I am and I'm not. It is a fully functioning collective that Peggy and I always like to refer to as a non-cooperative. It's more of a cooperative than it is a collective in that all you need to do to get your work shown is to show up at the Tuesday meeting and do your bit to help other people get their work shown and then you get to have a show. There's no artistic directorship, the whole programme is determined at one yearly retreat, there's some subsequent proposal periods that happen and the group decides on the proposals. We set that up in the eighties and it still functions that way. At the Tuesday evening meetings, everyone goes around and says what they're there for and what they'd like to get out of the place – not what I want to give, and we thought that was an essentially feminist thing to do. And that's how it kept from becoming something that was run by two or three people, that had two or three people's vision. It's also how we kept it in the eighties from becoming something where people just burned themselves out because they volunteered to serve coffee at night after that has been paid to be waitresses all day. And WOW still has the same issues: they still have the same battles around the place of men or now men in terms of trans men and trans women. There is a whole trans contingent who work at WOW and there's a large African American presence there too: WOW has developed into a much more diverse group than it was in the eighties, which is really thrilling. So I'm really proud of it. And it was a structure.

All of these structures create spaces for people to get to together to do something together. How does this relate to ideas of community?

It's about kinship. That word allows me to critique family and how it can be oppressive in different kinds of ways, particularly if you're a marginalised person like a queer person. What family means may be problematic. And I was thinking about community a lot – I like to think of it like a coalition. It's a group of people who come together for a particular period of time to do a thing and then that's it. It's not something you are part of for the rest of your life: it's not something that you have responsibility to maintain when it becomes completely not maintainable. It's about doing something with particular people, for a particular period of time, probably in a particular place. But it's around doing something. It doesn't last forever – that's the key.

That was my main lesson coming out of studying theatre

and becoming a political person – wanting to do and make something that changed something. When I was finding out about feminism, I was feeling kind of mystified about this intellectual concept of feminism. It was not until I worked with Spiderwoman that I realised it was the making something that made the feminism make sense. And then from thereon in I think I've never, ever had a group or a community that existed for its own sake, that was just about being together, being the same or having affinity: it was about making and doing something.

WOW came together because a group of people came together in 1980 to volunteer to make an international festival happen. After it happened, they wanted to do something else. Not they wanted to *be* something else, they wanted to *do* something else. And so we decided, Okay, well let's do that in a little shop front called WOW and then that became something more because it then became groups of people doing different things. And that became me teaching and so that was about how do I give people skills? And Split Britches is the same. All my feminism, all my activism, has not been around any kind of theory – it's really been around absolute practice. The minute the practice is backgrounded, not foregrounded, is when the thing starts to fall apart.

The other thing that I would like to say about community, and I will say this about relationships too: it's okay if they fall apart. You don't have to kill yourself to hold something together. I learned that from Spiderwoman in 1979. We were twelve women on the road. The youngest one was twenty-six, the oldest one, although we didn't know at the time, was practically sixty, three native American women, an African American woman from Harlem, one Irish working-class white woman, one southern working-class white woman, one lesbian and soon to be two other lesbians who came out. There was no way we were going to keep that thing together forever, even though in that moment, when it's good you want it to be forever. But there's no way. It has to be together for the particular period of time that it takes to do the thing you intend to do. And then you've got to let it go. That's how I've worked.

Hanging laundry in public and having people come up to me and talk to me about the public dirty laundry of the government or the shame of hanging private laundry in public, that's enough. Sometimes those little moments of engagement are moments of change – they are really powerful. When I was growing up in the rural south in the 1950s where racism – and homophobia – was so rampant, my early lessons around addressing racism were about slow exposure: just slowly chip away at the fear that people feel. Fear because they've not had the experience or not had the exposure or not had the conversation with others. To just try to chip away at that. So I think it came from that, those little moments of exposure were really important. But if you're going to change something you have to imagine it and sometimes those imaginations aren't on a world scale, they're on a street scale or a dinner table scale.

I'm not that interested in performance as an object or a conclusion. I'm interested in performance as a structure and what it allows people to do in the moment of making it and in the moment of performing it. Whether it's working with women in prison or teaching at university, people take responsibility for the performance space, for the moment, for the interaction with the audience. This taking of responsibility changes a person. What they do with that sense of taking responsibility is up to them – it could mean making more performance or just being more confident or doing something else.

Performance can be a structure that allows us to do things we wouldn't normally do: it is now or never. In that now, when you insert yourself into it, you are embodying things, doing things and moving things. You change in that: it *has* to be now or never.

2

'A marvellous experiment'[1] – exploring ideas of temporary community in a Magic Me intergenerational performance project

Sue Mayo

In Bhavesh Hindocha's documentary film about *Stepping Out in Stepney*, an intergenerational performance project, we see a lot of arrivals: older people clambering out of a minibus, children hurtling through the door of a drama studio and students from Queen Mary, University of London (QMUL), supporting older adult participants as they navigate the hurly burly of the entrance to their campus.

---

[1]A participant, commenting on the project, described it a 'a marvellous experiment'.

Stepping Out was the fourth in a series of performance projects designed and led by Magic Me, a London-based intergenerational arts organisation, in partnership with Ali Campbell, a Senior Lecturer in Performance at QMUL. Each of the four-generation performance projects included elders from a Jewish Care day centre; children from Osmani Primary School; undergraduate drama students; care and teaching staff; and artists including me, Ali Campbell, Julian West (musician), Bhavesh Hindocha (film-maker) and Keith Ellis (film-maker and musician). [2]

QMUL is in east London, an area with a rich history of immigration and an ethnically and socially diverse population. In 2012, over 16,000 students attended the university – the population of a small town. However, QMUL's extensive, well-resourced campus and the durational nature of student life limit their connections with the area's local inhabitants. For many students the focus of daily life is on campus and most people they encounter who are over thirty years old are staff. Each week, as I went to greet the children and the older people, I was fascinated to watch the impact of their arrival: their pace was different and they sometimes halted the students' accustomed flow of entry and exit to the university. Their voices brought in new tones and accents. They simply weren't usually in this space: they were stepping in. Once in the door, the group had come to meet and to make – to build relationships and to create a piece of performance together.

This chapter explores the ways in which arts practices developed by Magic Me connect the building of relationships with the creation of moments of and pieces of art. I examine Magic Me's robust yet delicate and detailed approach to the fostering of connectivity and dialogue as a foundational

---

[2]On both these projects film-makers were part of the artistic team. Present at many of the sessions the film-makers created documentaries of the work, partly as a way to include moments from the workshops in the performance, and partly to address the reality that the performance could never truly reflect all that had gone on in the room.

condition for creativity and risk-taking. I propose that these temporary groupings, the chunk of time, space and place that we call 'a project', is a temporary community. This is examined in the context of current discourse around the urban experience of inhabitants of a multi-cultural multi-faith city – what Peter Hall, Professor of Planning and Regeneration, describes as a 'dynamic polycentric city region'.[3] This dynamism is revealed through energy and inventiveness but also through tensions and anxiety about social cohesion. The understanding and experience of community is inevitably both crucial and contested in such a city.

In order to investigate the particular value in community that is temporary, I examine the ongoing fascination and difficulty with what Amit calls 'this idea and/or form of sociality that continues to so engage our attention'.[4] Zygmunt Bauman's work on community[5] helps me to navigate this contested but essential term and Kurt Lewin's Field Theory informs this analysis.

Field Theory is 'a set of principles, an outlook, a method, and a whole way of thinking that relates to the intimate interconnectedness between [...] events and the settings or situations in which these events take place'.[6] It is a phenomenological approach that has influenced Gestalt Therapy, particularly work with groups. Field Theory positions a group as individuals constantly in flux, constellating around internal and external needs or drives. The *field* consists of all the interactive phenomena of individuals and their environment and all aspects of that field are potentially significant and

---

[3]Peter Hall, *London Voices, London Lives: Tales from a Working Capital* (Bristol: The Policy Press, 2007), p. 8.
[4]Vered Amit (ed.), *Realizing Community: Concepts, Social Relationships and Sentiments* (London: Routledge, 2002), p. 1.
[5]Bauman, *Community*.
[6]Malcolm Partlett, 'Contemporary Gestalt Theraphy: Field Theory' in Ansel L. Woldt and Sarah M. Toman (eds), *Gestalt Therapy: History, Theory, and Practice* (London: Sage, 2005), pp. 41–64, 47.

FIGURE 3 *A workshop from* The Wisdom of All Ages *(2005).*
Photo: Magic Me.

interconnected. The field and the forces operating in the field
are all potentially alive and significant, but the perspective of
the field changes as the group organises and understands itself
differently from moment to moment. People actively organise
and reorganise their perception of their circumstances (or field)
by continually making some aspects of that field the focus, or
foreground, while others become background, and vice versa.
The need or interest of those in the group organises the field.[7]
This sense of clustering, of coming together temporarily but
meaningfully, is at the heart of what I want to explore.

The Wisdom of All Ages (2005) and *Stepping out in
Stepney* (2006), two intergenerational performance projects
developed by Magic Me, are my case studies. Through a close
reading of moments within these projects, I argue that it is in

---

[7]For further information see Jennifer Mackewn, *Developing Gestalt
Counselling* (London: Sage, 1997).

the detail of the interactions between all the people involved in these projects that we can see the enacting of connectivity that is the fabric of community. I am writing from the position of a theatre maker involved in both these projects and as an artist with a long involvement in intergenerational art practice, committed to reframing and reinvigorating the vocabulary that attaches itself to work with older people and to the discourse of evaluation and impact.

Magic Me

Magic Me was founded in the UK in 1989 by former graphic designer Susan Langford. Susan had been inspired by a meeting with Kathy Levin, founder of Magic Me in the USA, which brought together isolated older people with young people experiencing school exclusions or other challenging situations. The emphasis for Levin was on building relationships between one young and one older person, which would be mutually beneficial. Partnerships were built up over a sustained series of visits by the young person to the older person. Sometimes these visits took place over a number of years. This relationship building remained a central part of Langford's vision, but she reimagined it within the context of arts practice, making creative collaboration and exploration the meeting place.

In 1988 Margaret Thatcher, the Conservative Prime Minister, had been in post for nine years. Her emphasis on individual responsibility and on the Free Market Economy were by now embedded in British institutions. In an interview in *Woman's Own* in 1987 she stated that people seeking help from the state 'are casting their problems on society and who is society? There is no such thing! There are individual men and women.'[8] For many of us working in the arts at that time,

---

[8]Margaret Thatcher Foundation, Interview for *Woman's Own* ('No Such Thing as Society'), http://www.margaretthatcher.org/document/106689 (accessed 24 January 2012).

particularly those working in situations where the fractures in society were evident, this was an unsurprising but nonetheless startling view of the world: our work was often framed as a way of reconnecting, of mending tears, in order to build a stronger and more confident society.

In the three decades that Magic Me has been operating, there have been continued challenges to the idea and value of connectivity, relationship building, community and society. Young and older people are often the central focus of political concern whilst continuing to be on the margins of decision-making processes. Issues such as anti-social behaviour, a declining birth rate and an ageing population present real financial and societal challenges to government. In 1995 there were fewer than nine million people over 65 in the UK; by 2030 it is estimated that there will be thirteen million. The current financial crisis in Europe and North America highlights many governments' lack of preparation for this phenomenon and there are significant concerns about the social impact of this on individuals, families and communities.

Against this background, Magic Me has grown in both its scope and in the sheer variety of the ways in which it brings young and older people together for shared creative activity. Building relationships through arts practices continues to be of central importance. Employing a pool of artists, including theatre makers, musicians, dancers, photographers, film makers, and visual artists, supported through ongoing training and reflection, Magic Me continually develops the forms and sites in which this meeting can take place. In 2012, at the time of writing, projects using a range of art forms are running in day centres, schools, residential care homes, The Museum of Childhood and at The Women's Library. Three groups are preparing performance work to be staged at Wilton's Music Hall as part of a collaboration with experimental performance company Duckie. Others are creating a visual and audio installation for London buses about life on the Mile End Road as part of the city's Olympic celebrations. A group of women aged between 14 and 85 are creating films and podcasts as part of an event in the London International Festival of Theatre.

Based and primarily working in the London Borough of Tower Hamlets, the work encounters and includes people from diverse ethnic and faith identities and a wide range of economic backgrounds. Over half of Tower Hamlets' population are from non-white British ethnic groups. A third of these are Bangladeshi and, within this population, over a third are fifteen years old or younger. Tower Hamlets ranks as the third most deprived local authority in England and life expectancy for men and women in the Borough is one of the lowest in the country. In contrast to this picture of diversity and poverty, Tower Hamlets is also home to the global financial centres of Canary Wharf, thriving commercial districts, and Brick Lane, known for its Asian restaurants, shops and its alternative arts community. The contradiction and complexity of the borough is reflected, through the participants, in a Magic Me project.

Although recognised as a leader in its field internationally, Magic Me is embedded in East London. It remains a small organisation with a core team of four, and its pool of freelance artists (currently 27). From the particularity of its local commitment and knowledge, the work has grown and developed in ways that have a significance across a wide range of national and international settings, maintaining core values, and a commitment to this central activity of meeting and making, reflected in the projects from the very start.

Meeting places and making spaces

All the elders came on Tuesday. Those who had been before were really relaxed and at ease in the space – very pleased to be there. We had an opening circle for welcomes and introductions, and a look at our feet and shoes. When I first asked if you could tell people's age by their shoes, most people said no. And yet there were some really age specific shoes in that circle. So we pushed them a bit. Some of the adults talked about needing to have Velcro instead of laces, a feature that many of the children shared. But only the children had flashing lights in their shoes.

Then we worked in small groups of students, children and elders. Everyone had a look at a pair of shoes – we had brought in three pairs: children's leather boots, trainers, and red high heels. Each group looked at, reflected on, handled, played with and then created a narrative for those shoes. One group created and then told us the story of the little boy who had worn the boots; in another we heard the shoes speak. It was a lovely session – good chats, wonderful moments of connection.[9]

In this reflection from my journal I am aware of three strands that are key to the ways of working; making a 'home' space, allowing for commonalities and difference to emerge, and having a purpose.

Making a home space

While the students were 'at home' in QMUL, both elders and children were visiting the university from quite different spaces and places. We, the hosts, needed to pay attention to the housekeeping, to make sure we had tea and juice and good biscuits. On one project, every week, we borrowed a teaspoon from the university porter, and this ritual added to a sense of leaving our footprints on this space. The porter was, quite literally, the gatekeeper, and the transaction we enacted each week built a relationship with him. At the end of the project, he took time off work in order to see the performance.

---

[9]Sue Mayo, Stepping Out Project Diary, 7 and 8 October 2006.

Week by week the project allowed us to add another layer of knowledge and experience of that specific place. We became familiar with the room, the furniture, the view of the Mile End Road. As a team of artists we were intrigued to see that an adult in the group who had Alzheimer's, and did not remember having been in the room before, always visibly relaxed when she arrived. It was as if the repetition of visiting and the warm welcome from all the participants created a kind of exoskeleton: the room itself held the identity of the project and she was able to confidently enter this place layered with experiences.

I use the term community principally as a grouping of people constituted by relationship rather than by a shared identity that is externally given and accepted internally to varying degrees (for example through faith community or ethnicity). But it is relationship in convergence with place and with purpose. If we can begin to think about a group like this as a small community, it is partially because of place, it is situated. The group had a common connection to East London, but this was not to be taken for granted as a strong element in the building of relationship. The experiences of home in East London in the group were many and various: the students had two years of experience of studying rather than living in the area; the school children, like some of the adults, may have spent their entire lives in the area but would have entirely different relationships with it, its history and development. The project's home was this studio, a space they were making into a place, a temporary home. Significantly, for two of the groups this place was not a space related to being an older person or to being a child, like the day centre and school they had travelled from. No space is neutral, but here the elders and the children were away from a building that told everyone who they were. The students were on familiar territory, but one that was only temporarily theirs. The group was going to be building its own flexible identity.

Negotiating commonalities and differences

Sitting in a circle at the start of that session encouraged us to look carefully at one another. We did not just happen to be in the same room at the same time. *Who were we?* In a Magic Me project everyone knows there will be differences in the group before they start. Part of the practice is for the generations to meet separately beforehand to think about the others – to discover what we might already think and know, to get prejudgements on the table. The first meeting brings the reality into the room. *Who are we all?* There is no expectation of immediate bonding. Magic Me artists use a wealth of simple, introductory exercises (some of them created by the artists for the purpose) that can make the meeting possible. These activities are designed to help to build connection, to hear names, to find common ground; they are not designed to exclude difference. In my journal example, we looked at each other's shoes. It is simple to ask everyone to look at each other's shoes. But for some of the children any signs of ageing, like bulky, buniony feet, can be difficult and distressing. For an adult who used to go running, a pair of nice trainers can be an unwelcome reminder of infirmity. Being surprised that a teacher wears leopard-skin high heels is an opening to the possibility that everyone might surprise you, and you might surprise them. So the simple thing brings everyone in the group to a place of fun *and* delicacy. We see some of the differences and we still proceed to meet and to make something together.

If the circle told us something about the whole group, the small group brought our identities into focus. Names – some of which may be unfamiliar – to learn, different accents or deafness to accommodate. The group was meeting in order to make something together, so already in the early stages we were creating and sharing stories. The stories that emerged were mosaics, collages. The pair of shoes in each group created the exterior focus that became a lightning rod for imagination, for guesses and the sharing of experiences. I remember being very much aware that no one voice was dominant, not the voice of age and memory, not the voice of youth and playfulness. The intergenerationalness for me really means that everyone's voice and experience is equally present. This work reminds me again and again that memories don't only belong to older people or playfulness to the young. We are looking for structures that release everyone from the necessity to perform their age or gender or ethnicity. It opens up the possibility of expanding to express many different facets of being oneself. This can challenge not only assumptions about others, but our assumptions, and our learned behaviours, about ourselves. It can take time in a project for participants to let themselves off being older and wiser, or a spokesperson for their ethnicity or faith community. One adult participant from Jewish Care, interviewed in Hindocha's film, remarks with delight, 'It's ageless, classless, no ageism as such.'

Purpose

We might say then that this negotiated and made space allowed everyone the opportunity, if they wanted to take it, to move between the different senses of belonging that made up their identity. But the group was not there only for the meeting, but also for the making. The dynamic created by the intention to create a performance can sometimes be at odds with the needs of relationship building, but it also helps us to remember to be explorers, adventurers. Ali Campbell would often remind us all that if we started with everyone's limitations what we'd learn was their limitations. The call to create, to make something new, that *only we* as a group could make ensured that we continued to push ourselves and to be inventive. This gave the group a purpose. The sequence of activities I have just described is a metaphor for the whole process: the gathering into a circle to see who the group is; the deeper meeting, getting to know, negotiating and sharing stores; and then the turning outwards to tell the story, becoming an audience and witness to each other, in preparation for the public audience who will come. The artist Jan Stirling, who worked with Magic Me for several years, expressed it in this way: 'Meeting *is* making.' She saw that the relationship building and the creation of work were inextricably connected and co-dependent.

Neighbourliness

These themes of connectivity, building together and managing difference need to all be seen against the backdrop of the city in which they take place. In *London Voices, London Lives: Tales from a Working Capital* (2007) Peter Hall summarises and analyses interviews with hundreds of Londoners over a three-year period. He describes London as unique: unique because of its multi-ethnic, multi-cultural nature, its sheer spread, and the fact that, unlike any other UK city, it is still growing. Out of the interviews emerge some findings that are of relevance to this investigation of temporary community. Despite nostalgia for what is perceived to be a sense of community that has disappeared, the interviewers found neighbourliness to be in good working order. But its boundaries are important. You do what you can for your neighbours, but you don't have to be friends. On the whole, inhabitants of the city know how to rub along together, how to make life go smoothly, through small, reciprocal gestures – taking in a parcel, feeding a neighbour's pet and so on. But the next stage, getting to know people and being known, is a much harder task. One interviewee expresses the difficulty of getting further than this rubbing along together:

> I don't know how you find out about other people, I think everybody just do their own thing and try to be, you know,

good neighbours, or good people, not neighbours [...] but neighbourliness [...] I haven't had much to do with my, you know, neighbours [...] the property is rented so and the tenants change very frequently.[10]

Hall found that feeling part of a community meant 'fitting in', being recognised and part of a network of relationships.[11] A day centre manager in Tower Hamlets reiterated this when he told me that isolation, not poverty, was the biggest problem among older people locally. Achieving a sense of belonging is often not an easy, spontaneous thing. It is built and shaped. It requires opportunities to come into relationship with others. There are many groupings, accidental and purposeful that can provide the opportunities to connect. In my own life these include my work, my book group, neighbours, friends, people I know through my child's school, people I have got to know through walking my dog. None of these are isolated or self-contained, there are crossovers, but they all need some form, some purpose, some desire which brings me into contact with others. They are not tightly boundaried – in each there is space for difference within the commonality. They do not have the same shape that an arts project brings, a shape created by boundaries that are temporal and locational. Bauman writes about the struggle to make and achieve unity in a world where there has been 'a breach in the protective walls of community.'[12] Does an arts project, with its clearly defined parameters, provide a 'protective wall'? If we take as our guidance the three aspects that Hall identifies in the interviews with Londoners, of feeling part of, being recognised, and having relationships with others, the kind of community we are talking about is not about sameness. Perhaps in a temporary community, in particular one that

---

[10] Hall, *London Voices, London Lives*, p. 356.
[11] Ibid., p. 310.
[12] Bauman, *Community*, p. 13.

FIGURE 4 The Wisdom of All Ages *performance, 2005. Photo: Julia Illmer, Magic Me.*

everyone knows is temporary, like a project, the group conspire together to find enough in common between them to allow them to discover their differences without losing the sense of group. The group is not struggling to define a collective identity, because the purpose of the project, the making of a performance in this case, provides an external identity, and a dynamic, carrying the group from its early meeting towards its ending. The group is free to co-create the internal identity. This structure, the container for the building of relationship, is important. The group may hide difficult or fearful feelings about one another in order to keep a good atmosphere, but relationships will remain casual if assumptions and difficulties are ignored.

Beyond surface

Hall identifies celebration of and difficulty with difference as the dual themes of London:

> Many Londoners celebrate the fact that theirs is one of the most racially and culturally diverse cities on earth [...] But, when it comes down to the neighbourhoods where Londoners live their lives, it gets more complicated.[13]

His research highlights the great difficulties that individuals can have with one another. Race, class and rapid change are the most aggravating factors identified by the interviewees. Hall identifies nostalgia for the past – 'I don't think they'll ever have what we had – a sense of belonging. Cause we did belong.'[14] This sense of un-sureness, of change, is echoed by Bauman: 'walls are far from solid and most certainly not fixed once and for all; eminently mobile they remind the traveller-through-life of cardboard partitions or screens meant to be repositioned over and over again'.[15]

Bauman's reference to Henning Bech's idea that in crowded urban situations we become 'surfaces' only to one another[16] reminds me of a comment that Langford made – that she wanted to leave design as she was 'fed up with surface work'.[17] But when the crowdedness also includes visible difference, in terms of age and ethnicity, when the international, national and, sometimes, domestic script describes antagonistic Jewish/Islamic relationships, and when many families live at geographical distances that limit contact between generations, the possibility and the desire to go beyond the surface can be limited.

---

[13] Hall, *London Voices, London Lives*, p. 407.

[14] Interviewee in ibid., pp. 372–3.

[15] Bauman, *Community* p. 45.

[16] Ibid., p. 147.

[17] Susan Langford, e-mail to Sue Mayo, 26 January 2012.

Magic Me, like other arts- and community-based organisations, aims to create 'protective walls' within which connection and co-creation can occur. Within these there is room for a 'marvellous experiment'. It was after some years of refining the practice, of experimentation and discovery that Langford decided to try to articulate some of what was emerging as intergenerational practice. As the field of work grew and became more recognised, it became important to distil and communicate what was being learned on the ground. In 2001 she invited me to co-write a handbook on intergenerational arts practice – *Sharing the Experience*. For Langford, one of the motivating forces for articulating and publishing the practice that had been developed was the frequency with which she heard the assumption that intergenerational work was somehow easy, that there would be a natural bond between young people and adults who could, from a purely age perspective, be their grandparents. We both knew that the work took very careful and detailed design, setting up and delivery. What do both groups, and the organisations to which they are connected, expect and hope for? What are the fears and assumptions about one another? What is the best place to meet – a place that can provide this special, equally accessible territory for meeting? The book became a very practical guide, taking the reader from the initial idea through to the end of a project. It also provided an opportunity to look at what the detail of the practice might reveal. When, in Magic Me's work, groups meet before the project to think about what they expect, anticipate and fear, I have heard adults complain about how children push them aside in bus queues, and I have heard young people make exactly the same complaint about adults. I have heard children polarise the qualities and weaknesses they foresee in their older partners as being, on the one hand, very wise and empathetic and, on the other, very fragile and very bossy. It is quite possible in Tower Hamlets to find white adults who don't know anyone from the Bangladeshi community, and I have met young Bangladeshis who didn't know that any Jewish people lived in

London. Often the groups are curious about one another, but people can be fearful too. Many of the students involved in the projects at Queen Mary expressed fears related to their own feelings in relation to grandparents, including feelings of guilt that grandparents lived in care homes. So the first meeting can be difficult as well as intriguing. The tone of the session is important, and it is through arts structures that the group finds a way to start meeting, beyond the surfaces.

On The Wisdom of all Ages we, as artists, were interested in the wisdom (that is to say the knowledge gained and honed through experience) present at every age. Because we were also interested in how this wisdom got shared, we used the idea and practice of learning and teaching throughout the project. We taught the children to make flamboyant name badges before they met the other participants, and then they taught the students how to do it. They all taught the older adults, and our reflection on that session illuminates a meeting that went beneath the surface.

Joshua (a shy man from Jewish Care) was playing with some feathers, which he hadn't used for his name badge. He was sitting with Saif, a boy who isn't too sure about the project. Joshua wasn't looking too good today – he bites his nails to the quick. Not embarrassed by his nails, he began to play. He turned his feathers into a moustache and allowed himself to be photographed. This started a conversation with Saif about eyebrows, moustaches and beards. Saif talked to Joshua about his dad, his beard and shaving. These two were connecting through talking about being a man.[18]

The activity provided a very slender structure. What happened within that was completely particular to these two people, both of whom were slightly at the edge of the group. This

---

[18] Sue Mayo, The Wisdom of all Ages Project Diary, 27 September 2005.

relationship between the offer from the artists, of a clear but
open structure, which can then be filled by the questioning
and the answers of the participants, is central to Magic Me's
practice. Equally important is that no participant is being
favoured by the content. The material gives everyone a chance
to speak and to listen, to teach and to learn. In *The Wisdom of
All Ages* we asked everyone in the group to tell us something
that they could teach the group. This extraordinary list became
a part of the final show, spoken directly to the audience.

There are so many things you could learn from all of us.
For example we could teach you
Respect and loving kindness, or
How to make a boat out of newspaper.

Patience,
Machining,
How to grow a sunflower.
How to conquer your nerves
and how to yodel.

We could show you
How to dance in an African Party,
How to clean a horse's teeth,
How to cook the best roast dinner,

the patience to finish a crossword,
the ten commandments, especially 'love thy neighbour as
thyself',
never mind the religion.

You could learn
Chinese,
To ski,
To dance the Gay Gordon's,
To make beautiful labels
and to have fun.

To draw an aeroplane and to build an aeroplane.

We could show you
Patience,
How to make triple chocolate brownies,
How to stop someone from making your baby cousin cry,
and horse jumping.

You could learn to cut hair,
To get along with other people,
To try to learn new things,
To paint
and to get your head to touch your feet, backwards.

We could show you how to be patient, friendly and to
listen.
To treat others as you want to be treated,
To be good,
To giggle.
We would show you by example.

We could teach you
bee language,
to sail a boat,
to cook a brilliant roast dinner,
to accessorise.

We could teach you
new songs.

There is nothing in here that confines older people to the past
and their memories, the students to being young, cool and
'street', or the children to being cute. The meeting place is rich
with everyone's experiences, but it is being newly minted. This
list could only have been made by these people.

As the group grows beyond the 'surfaces' in their meeting
together and making together, they become, at first, neighbourly.

The project works through small acts of reciprocal kindness and mutuality. The next stage, making real connections, is not about becoming homogeneous, or about unity. It happens when the sense of connection is robust enough it for the differences to emerge. In *Stepping out in Stepney* there was an interesting encounter between a Bangladeshi Muslim boy of eight and one of the artists. The boy said to the artist, who is white, 'You are a Christian.' The artist responded that he wasn't and there was a gentle tug of war for some time before it became possible for the younger disputant to let go of his fixed understanding and make room in his worldview for a white man who wasn't Christian. Using what Parlett calls the 'informing metaphor' of Field Theory, we see that the field contains our history and hopes, our habits, attitudes and influences, jostling to come to the foreground. The time that the artist gave to this conversation and his gentle refusal to collude with a fixed view allowed the young participant to shift both his view of the other and his own system of judgement. Of course, the child's worldview came from both internal and external influences, and Parlett reminds us that these 'in practice are all interacting and affecting each other. They "come together" and to try to take them apart and study them one at a time and independently means falling into the reductionist trap.'[19] Understanding can move the shape of the constellation or grouping, and these small transactions reveal the importance of moments of going 'beyond the surfaces' and becoming more real to one another. An artist working on another Magic Me project reflected on the apparent simplicity and the actual potential depth of this building of relationship,

> even doing a project I still feel I have only a shadowy outline of what it all means, doing this work. I got such

---

[19] Malcolm Partlett, 'Contemporary Gestalt Therapy: Field Theory' in Ansel L. Woldt and Sarah M. Toman (eds), *Gestalt Therapy: History, Theory and Practice* (London: Sage, 2005), pp. 41–64, 46.

a lot out of the project I worked on. When the pairs came together, some worked and for some it seemed difficult. It is very exciting and, I have a sense, revolutionary! I think it's really about forging relationships through the walls.[20]

Improvising identity

Although much of the meeting in a Magic Me project happens through encounters between pairs – particularly an adult and a young person – the sense of growing community is revealed most in the life of the group. Keith Ellis, one of the artists, commented, 'It seemed to put things back into balance, having all the ages together. You don't notice the separation until you get them all together – then it feels right.' Keith was talking about seeing a room full of different ages, genders, ethnicities, faith allegiances, roots come together and play together. 'This is how the world should be,' he added. I am aware that photographs of the work and the work itself often evoke a sense of relief in the viewer, a sense that our society is not that divided after all. Or perhaps it eases an anxiety that differences between people are irreconcilable. This sense of relief is also present for participants, who can sometimes express their sadness at being cut off from people of other ages and backgrounds who live in the same locality.

When the children aren't there I feel that something is missing. When I don't know where they are I feel worried. When I see them, everything comes back together.[21]

---

[20] Catherine Goldstein, CPD Feedback, e-mail to Susan Langford, 20 August 2005.
[21] Comment made by adult participant with Alzheimer's in a Magic Me project in 2004.

We must be cautious of idealising these particular moments, although they help us to see the connections that we aspire to. But the group is in constant development and grows as aspects of the various identities in the room are revealed and playfully questioned.

The following two examples reveal this shifting sense of the fluidity of identity. Children who arrived at a session with hennaed hands, because they had been to a wedding, were amazed to discover how many people in the group knew what the henna was, how it was done, and had had it done themselves. They were used to being 'other' to non-Bangladeshi people and were surprised when this sense of themselves was reconfigured. A teaching assistant came to both projects to support a child with a learning disability. She expected to be entirely responsible for Suman's support and spoke about feeling 'flattered, moved and grateful' when she realised that she could share this responsibility, that others in the room had knowledge and experience that meant they could also support him too, and that they wanted to learn from her and from him. The group, the community, enabled her to participate in the projects rather than be on the periphery of them. Both examples revealed the possibility for the group to experiment and improvise with individual and group identity.

Group and constellation

The work that we are doing together, sharing personal and fictional stories, improvising, editing and discarding, trying new things and showing our expertise in familiar things is dynamic and cumulative. Even without the impetus of the performance, the group created increasing points of contact. Writing about the application of Field Theory to group work, Parlett quotes Hunter Beaumont:

Contact is not passive perception of a fixed objective

reality, but rather the creation of a phenomenal experimental reality [...] Contact is [...] a mutually creative interaction.[22]

Lewin articulated Field Theory as a way of understanding groups. If we apply this to the nature of the group that is at the heart of a Magic Me project, it illuminates something provocative about community and individual identity. In the projects I focus on here, we chose to bring together three groups of people, two chosen by age, who also brought faith identities. The elders were all Jewish and the children were all Muslim. The third group was made up of undergraduate students, aged between nineteen and twenty-two. All of the children and elders lived in Tower Hamlets; some of the students did. The artists were the fourth generational group. All this information is part of the field, but it's not the only information. Part of the development of the group *as* a group, as a community, is to begin to unfold the diversity within each named group, to discover commonalities, connections and common purpose. One way of looking at this is to say that this happens as the need and interests of the group reconfigure the field.

In these projects, this configuring describes how the group are seeing themselves as a group, but also seeing themselves *being seen* as a group – what they experience and show. An exercise where we mapped the local streets configured the field in one way; singing together allowed another figure to emerge. When the adults arrived straight from a Hanukkah celebration it was different from the day when we met to talk about costumes. And the artists are not outside the field. They bring with them potentially significant elements (gender, ethnicity, age for example) and it is not only their instructions, guidance or interventions that configure the field at any given moment.

---

[22] Parlett, 'Contemporary Gestalt Therapy', p. 47.

This sense of constant change and refocusing underlines the improvisational aspect of this work. There are clear plans and a desired end product, but who the group are, and how they are must be attended to and responded to: this is always. During one of the final sessions in the run up to the performance of *Stepping Out in Stepney*, we had planned to rehearse key scenes. However, when the group arrived, they seemed tired and missed the times they had had to chat in the earlier sessions. We re-planned the session rapidly and worked on making some props. As Nevis reminds us, 'The general shift in direction away from anything like fixed techniques is an indication of the need to attend to the organisation of the field as it is encountered in the moment.'[23] The participants worked in small groups, busy but calm, chatting and laughing, re-establishing relationships. This was a risky strategy – we missed an important rehearsal – but if we believe that the quality of relationships between people informs the quality of the performance, we ran a much greater risk if we ignored what the group was telling us it needed.

Between nostalgia and utopia – negotiating Tower Hamlets' identities

Within Tower Hamlets much of the population lives in isolated islands, not just between ethnically identified communities, but *within* those communities.

The East End of London has a number of identities caught as much in the stories of the Blitz, or the curry houses of Brick Lane, as in the architecturally revealed layers of immigration – the Huguenot chapel that became a synagogue and then a mosque, for example. Michael Young and Peter Wilmott's

---

[23] Edwin C. Nevis, *Organizational Consulting: A Gestalt Approach* (New York: Gardner Press, 1987), p. 49.

influential book *Family & Kinship in East London* (1957), based on interviews conducted in Bethnal Green, describes a working-class community responding to the struggles of low pay and limited opportunity by forming strong networks of mutual help and support. It warned against the effects of centralised planning systems that advised the clearance of slums and the dispersal of inhabitants, regardless of familial and neighbourly ties. It described a poor but cohesive community. Yet East London also has a history of ethnic and religious disturbance, from the march of the Blackshirts on Cable Street in 1936 to the activities of the English Defence League in the area in the past few years. It has known anti-Semitism and Islamophobia. The UK's first far-right local councillor, Derek Beackon, was elected to the Isle of Dogs in 1990. Poverty and wealth sit side by side, and, as the site of arrival for many waves of immigration, Tower Hamlets has seen friction as well as solidarity.

Understanding this broader historical socio-geographical landscape allows us to reframe Magic Me's work within it. The small, temporary communities developed through its work carries everything from 'outside' whilst being able to experiment with being different in a space that is new to participants and being newly configured by them. This distils all that is potential in this work. In a café scene in *Stepping out in Stepney*, a head waiter, played by diminutive Ahmed, throws out a cantankerous old customer, played by Simon. This scene provoked a warm and laughter-filled response; there was huge enjoyment at seeing the small in stature defeat the big. Also present in the room was the knowledge that many Jewish people have seen 'their' cafés disappear as a new community has become the head chef, and the knowledge that the children in the group were likely to outlive the older people. The performance space is redolent of so many layers of narrative. Perhaps one of the most important aspects of the work, in relation to ideas of social cohesion, is that it reminds all those involved that, as Lucy Lippard writes, 'Community doesn't mean understanding everything about everybody and resolving all the differences; it means knowing how to work within differences as they change and evolve.'[24] The relationships that emerge in a project are not dependent on agreement or negating tensions. In particular, artists may have to negotiate a sense of tension between the nostalgic – the longing for sense of community that is perceived to be damaged by the challenges of contemporary urban life – and the utopic, striving towards making significant future change in individuals, groups and society through our work. It is helpful to remember that within the project space we have both the past – as remembered now – and the future – as anticipated now – in a dynamic relationship. In this example, a created moment of fiction allowed for both the intended and the unintended resonances to have their place, safely.

The performance event in *Stepping Out in Stepney* and *The Wisdom of All Ages* were significant moments in the life of the group. In both cases, university timetabling demands meant that the group could not work in the theatre before the day of performance and we were aware of a sense of dislocation in our relocation to the space. When the scheduled performance time of *Wisdom* clashed with lunchtime at the Jewish Care Centre, their chefs arrived at QMUL with a full kosher three-course dinner, which the adults sat down and ate at properly laid tables with prayers before the meal. It also happened to be open day at the university, so they shared their lunch space with a bemused group of potential students and their parents. The community of the Day Centre became figural in the field for a time, but the group had to return to the performance space. The decision was made to keep the house-lights up a little so that the performers could see their audience. One adult performer remarked, 'I could see they were looking at me warmly and so I felt warm to them and it just went on like that.'[25]

---

[24] L. R. Lippard, *The Lure of the Local: Senses of Place in a Multicentered Society* (New York: The New Press, 1997), p. 24.
[25] Sue Mayo, e-mail journal, 10 December 2006.

Neither of the performances was free from surprise. After singing a solo Simon decided he would rather sit with the audience, and he stayed there until his next cue. When a performer didn't turn up we asked Alison, who drove the elders to rehearsal in the centre minibus, to take on the role. Because she had always been part of the process, she was able to step in without trouble. It would be fair to say that we, as a team of artists, were unsurprised by surprises, and indeed we valued them. Both performances included film that revealed the process of working together we had all been involved in, and we believed that, while we were looking for strong and engaging performance, we were not concealing who we were. Our temporary community could well be described in the way Lippard describes geographical communities – 'bumpily layered and mixed, exposing hybrid stories that cannot be seen in a linear fashion, aside from those "preserved" examples which usually stereotype and oversimplify the past'.[26]

Before the performance, Ali Campbell used the metaphor of tapestry to describe what the audience was about to encounter – often the back of a tapestry is a confusion of crossing threads – seeing both front and back of the performance. This was important because we didn't want the group to perform integration and harmonious diversity by hiding different energies and identities. Nonetheless, the performances where the groups turned outwards towards others depended on the mutual trust and enjoyment, the playfulness and the seriousness within this group. Audiences responded with comments including: 'That was a truly lovely and moving performance. Everyone looked like they had so much fun communicating and playing with each other. Thank you for sharing it with us – a great piece of community work.'

---

[26] Lippard, *The Lure of the Local*, p. 24.

Conclusion

Perhaps the biggest challenge to the idea that a project like this can create a kind of community is its temporariness. Does the worth of a community lie in its longevity? Bauman suggests that this is the weakness of the brief life of a community within a project.

> One thing which the aesthetic community does not do is to weave between its adherents a web of *ethical responsibilities*, and so of *long-term commitments*. Whatever bonds are established in the explosively brief life of the aesthetic community, they do not truly bind.[27]

However, in response to this, I am drawn again to the celebration of the present moment that Field Theory illuminates. After thirty years of practice, I have begun to feel wary of over-claiming the impact of socially engaged theatre practice, and feel much more drawn to the quality of what is going on within a project. I want to pay real attention to the small but significant transactions between people, to seeing them surprise themselves and be surprised by the other. As Nevis says, 'future events, planned or fantasised, are not given special status (as 'goals' or 'incentives') but again are seen as part of what is occurring in the present'.[28] Value does not only reside in the future, in what we will become, what will be left to the future, but also in the integrity and delight of what is possible now through a temporary community of individuals who create together something that only they could.

During the life of a project we saw many changes. An older woman who had been using her Zimmer frame more for moral support rather mobility left it at the day centre after a few weeks. A man who was usually silent began to talk.

---

[27] Bauman, *Community*, p. 71.
[28] Nevis, *Organizational Consulting*, p. 49.

Shy girls taught everyone how to dance. A boy with Down's Syndrome learned how to film. One of the students articulated something of this process:

> Jen talked about feeling sad when Joan spoke of her loneliness. Ali asked her about her feelings and she spoke about her fears for her own old age. We talked about the place of projects in people's lives. What are the ethics of a time-limited programme? We talked about what remains for participants when a project is over – the way the project builds confidence, builds capacity in the individual. That experience is indelible.[29]

Individual confidence is not the only important thing. The growth of the sense of group, of interconnected people who are responsive to one another is also crucial. Hall's interviews in *London Lives* identified something in successful communities in London; they were places that 'contained mobile and inclusive types of people who positively liked change and variety', unlike less-successful communities where people 'were suspicious and inward-looking and defensive of traditional ways of life'.[30]

Projects like the Magic Me ones described, reflect Hall's observations, provide a space in which to discover how to be outward looking and interested.

It may be that the very temporariness of a project encourages the individuals within it to experiment with connecting to people who look and sound different, who move differently, who have different histories; it is a place to learn to be more mobile, more able to move beyond the front door of one's habitual identity to discover who else you might be, who else you might meet.

Whilst the structure of these projects creates a strong framework within which different generations could meet and

---

[29] Sue Mayo, The Wisdom of All Ages Project Diary, 8 October 2006.
[30] Hall, *London Voices, London Lives*, p. 468.

make together, the connectivity goes beyond those 'protective walls'. The field is much bigger than a project, but the 'marvellous experiment' of making community allows us to see what we might be able to do and be, individually and collectively.

3

Mojisola Adebayo

Interview and introduction by Caoimhe McAvinchey

Mojisola Adebayo is a British born Nigerian–Danish performer, playwright, director, producer, workshop leader and teacher. Over the past twenty years she has worked on theatre projects across the world, from Antarctica to Zimbabwe.

Her diverse work has ranged from being an actor with the Royal Shakespeare Company to being a co-founding trainer of VIDYA, a slum dwellers' theatre company in Ahmedabad, India. Mojisola is a trustee and former member of Cardboard Citizens, Britain's only professional homeless people's theatre company, and is an Associate Artist for Pan Intercultural Arts. Having trained extensively with and also worked alongside Augusto Boal, she is a specialist facilitator in Theatre of the Oppressed, often invited to work in areas of conflict and crisis. All of her work is concerned with power, identity, personal and social change.

Mojisola has taught extensively at institutions including Goldsmiths, Rose Bruford, Manchester University, St Mary's and Trinity College, Dublin. Her PhD at QMUL examined *Afri-Queer Theatre: Challenging Homophobia, Re/Presenting*

Black Lesbians and Creative Performances Spaces for Black Queer Togetherness.

Mojisola's critically acclaimed plays include *Moj of the Antarctic: An African Odyssey* (2006), *Muhammad Ali and Me* (2008), *Desert Boy* (2010), *I Stand Corrected* (2012) and *48 Minutes for Palestine* (2010), a collaboration with Ashtar Theatre Palestine, that has toured the world.

* * *

Your practice covers an extraordinary range of work – you are a writer, performer, mentor, teacher, trainer and activist. What projects are you currently engaged in?

I am working on a production called *I Stand Corrected*, which is a collaboration with a South African dance artist called Mamela Nyamza. We met about four years ago when I was working in South Africa. We were interested in each other, drawn to each other. I'm interested in attraction … it's something that we don't talk about very much in this field when we think about community. But we were attracted to each other's work and to each other's experience, to each other's histories – to what we had in common and also what was so radically different. We live on two different continents and have had very different kinds of upbringings. But what we have in common is that we're both lesbian women, we're both black women, we both worked as independent artists and our work has a very real political commitment. It is very connected with the communities that influence and are affected by it. So we swapped DVDs, got really excited by each other's work and identified an area, an issue, that we both wanted to address: so-called corrective rape – the incidence of lesbian women being raped and usually murdered and the perpetrators justifying it on the basis that those women need to be corrected, straightened, to be made heterosexual. We wanted to respond to that subject.

I was also interested in the debates here in Britain at the moment around equal marriage. It is a violent idea that gay and lesbian people's love and commitment is not equal to heterosexuals' love and commitment. It's a dehumanising concept. I was interested in how these violent ideas and acts, and the colonial histories between South Africa and Britain, connect. So we created this piece, *I Stand Corrected*, and we performed it in Artscape Theatre Centre in Cape Town in 2012.

Part of the devising process for the show has been workshops with black lesbian women from various different townships around Cape Town. Mamela and I shared some of the ways in which we'd been working and the women shared their spirits, voices and stories. We wanted them in the show somehow but in a very real way. So their recorded voices, singing, open and close the show.

This work is very connected with a project that I'm very privileged to have been involved in. It's a group called Shout!, which is a – here come all the words – black, Asian, minority, ethnic, refugee, lesbian, gay, bi-sexual, transgender, queer, inter-sex (BAMERLGBTQI) youth arts, youth theatre group. It is based at Ovalhouse but very much connected with Talawa Theatre as well.[1] This group of young people is working through spoken word, creative writing and drama, indirectly exploring their cultural and queer experience.

---

[1]Ovalhouse has a rich history of socially engaged programming from its early beginnings as a sports venue for disadvantaged young people in the 1930s through to being at the vanguard of experimental theatre of the 1960s and 1970s, from supporting emerging gay and lesbian and women's theatre in the 1970s and 1980s through to the development of new Black and Asian writing in the 1990s. Part of its current artistic policy is to support 'performance that unpicks the social fabric of the city and uses it to make hang gliders to show us what it looks like from up there' (www.ovalhouse.com). Talawa Theatre Company, founded in 1986, was created in response to the lack of creative opportunities for actors from minority ethnic backgrounds and the general marginalisation of black peoples from cultural processes. It has, over the past three decades, developed work informed by black British experience, from the commissioning of new plays through to an extensive participation and education programme.

FIGURE 5 *Mojisola Adebayo and Mamela Nyamza in* I Stand Corrected. *Photo: Taryn Burger.*

I'm kind of an honorary elder member, a mentor. Mostly I try to be present in a supportive way, to not dominate the space, because it's led by a young person. I'm there partly just to be an older black queer person in the room, saying, by my presence, we're okay, we grow up, we get older and, hopefully, you'll be okay and you can be creative and expressive and who you are.

The group will come and see the show, *I Stand Corrected*, I will do workshops with them and that will influence us and will influence them. I'm hoping that the group doesn't stay as a closed group but that members from it may well come and join a production that I'm making with Talawa Theatre next year, the Talawa Young People's Theatre Project (TYPT). They may or may not be out and that's up to them, but that piece will be also exploring sexuality and gender in the context of race. So that's what I'm doing this year and next and points to how I relate performance and community, that those things are very, very integrated.

What's really interesting about this snapshot overview is what is underneath – an enormous amount of negotiation, time, trust and relationship building between people. Shout!, based at Ovalhouse, is located in a specific geographical community of south-east London but reaches beyond this to individuals who come together around questions of identity. It raises lots of really provocative questions about communities of identity – who is identified, who self-identifies and, by coming together to make something, what does that mean?

If anybody were to walk into the Shout! workshop last night who didn't know anything about the group and tried to figure out what community was happening, what issue they were working on, they couldn't be sure. And that's one of the beauties of it.

There's one young person who, when she walks down the street, probably nobody would recognise her as black, but she identifies as mixed heritage black – she just happens to have very, very light skin. She's often not recognised for her blackness and, because she's very feminine, she is often not recognised for her queerness. She is working alongside a very religious and very faithful Christian, black young man, who isn't out. What have the two of them got in common? And there's a very open and out son of a female transvestite who also happens to be gay and mixed heritage. What have they got in common? And what are we doing in the workshop, telling stories about heroes? What is the project really? But all of us, me included, feel immense pleasure at being in the space with other people who know what it is to feel in a minority *within* a minority. Last night one of the members turned to another couple of women who are coming along regularly now and just said, I'm so glad you're here. And it's just a mutual feeling of, I'm really happy to be in this room with all of you. And that's enough. I have never felt so relieved, comforted, supported – possibly even healed – in a group that I'm partly facilitating. I'm forty-one years old and feel so lucky because this is the group I needed at fourteen but never had, and I'm in it now. To be different because of race and sexuality – those things are so enormous in terms of how they impact on your sense of yourself living in Britain at the moment. The fact that they're in a minority within a minority means that it feels really good when you're in a space with other people who get it and you don't have to explain those details, you can express yourself creatively without feeling judged or laughed at. It's about what we *don't* say in that space, what we don't have to explain, it's a relief.

What was the invitation offered which brought this group of individuals together? And is there an assumption that the work you make is about that sense of being a minority within a minority – or is it more open, less explicit, than that?

The invitation to be part of Shout! is around all of those identities within the acronym of BAMERLGBTQI and it's interesting who understands what by that. Originally, on the Ovalhouse website, I think it was around sexual and racial diversity, and that was partly to protect the members because not all of them are out. So we got quite a lot of phone calls from people who didn't really know what that meant but wanted to join a theatre group. And the young leader of the project had to have lots of conversations with young people on the phone about their sexuality, but without making them feel uncomfortable. But what's really clear is that even though they have all got something around sexual and racial diversity in common we don't particularly *talk* a great deal about sexuality. People come along because they want to express themselves creatively – that's the most important thing. To do some creative, expressive work – but not necessarily with a particular end in sight – is wonderful. We're finding out what the work's going to be about and what forms the group is attracted to. There's been a lot of creative writing: that seems to be what people are really responding to, but there is no agenda in terms of the topic that we explore.

Where did the impetus for creating this particular space to be and work together come from?

It was the young leader who identified that need as a young, black, mixed-heritage, lesbian woman. She did some research and talked to The Albert Kennedy Trust which is a charity for young gay, lesbian, bisexual homeless people. Around sixty per cent of their calls come from black and minority ethnic young people, which is completely disproportionate with the wider population. A worker from the Albert Kennedy Trust said, you need to do something to address this, you need to do something using your skills in the arts. So the young leader spoke with the Head of Participation at Ovalhouse. I also said that I've always wanted to set up a youth theatre for this kind of group – whatever that group is – and she then connected us. But it's the young leader's project. It's really crucial that it's led by a young person with support from older, more experienced people.

So far we've had about eight sessions. In a few weeks there's a sharing, a live night performance. That'll be interesting to see how that goes, around being out and not being out, and who you get up in front of. And then I'm going to mentor the young leader, mainly on sustainability fundraising – that's going to be my main role from here on in – so that she can keep the group going regularly. I think it's going to become a kind of experimental performance group as opposed to a kind of weekly youth theatre.

You have made particular choices about the work that you make and the commissions that you take: I'm curious about how this body of work informs or challenges your understanding of 'community' and what is expected of that word.

The idea I come back to when I think about community is, what do we have in *common*? Fundamentally, we all have something in common, there's not a person on this planet that I couldn't find something in common with. So, at the risk of sounding really wishy-washy, we are a global community. But

I really do believe that. And then there are other questions – why do we choose each other? Or why are we chosen to be together? Why does somebody say, I *need* to be with these people in this context? And I think what I'm most drawn to, although this isn't always very transparent, are the projects where people have said, I'd like to be together with those people – a bit like Shout! I've always been reticent about working on projects where I'm not clear that people have chosen to be together, which is why I don't do a great deal of work in schools or prisons. Not that I don't respect that, I do respect it enormously, but I'm attracted to those projects where there's a genuine desire from inside a group to do something together.

And maybe in a way that goes back to the question about attraction and Mamela, my collaborator on *I Stand Corrected*. We genuinely wanted to be together in our own mini community.

If I was to looking for contradictions now, and thinking about my work with Cardboard Citizens, I suppose there are other kinds of communities where people look around and go, oh look, we're together, shall we do something? We're in this hostel, they're doing a workshop downstairs, shall we go? Are you going? I'll go. Or, I'm in this workshop in the basement of the hostel in Mare Street ... Who else is here? Do I want to stay? Do I want to be in the same room as these people? Is this fun? Am I getting pleasure? Do I feel better at the end than I did at the beginning? So, sometimes those things are quite accidental. And sometimes, when there's a big outside agenda of putting people together when there hasn't been a great deal of negotiation about that, that worries me.

The distinction between the desire *to be together or the recognition that we* happen *to be together is interesting. You've worked in places that have been fractured by war, by social inequity, by racism, where people live alongside rather than with each other. Sometimes performance is asked to negotiate*

differences between people, to mend or make a community.
What has your experience in different community contexts
helped you think about the possibilities or limitations of
performance?

The act of performing is a moment of declaration: we, the
performers, have been working together and we're going to
show you, the audience, what we've been doing. In doing
that, we are going to open up the restrictions of community –
what it is and who defines and shapes it. And in that process,
I'm going to learn something as a performer, a performance
maker, and the audience is going to learn something, not in
formal educational terms, but in things moving you, taking
you somewhere.

In any rehearsal room or community centre or youth club
that you're making a piece of work, the moment that you open
that out to an audience serves a really important function in
terms of dialogue, reflection, of breaking down barriers. This
is not to negate the importance of process. In 1997, I worked
on a project with Pan Intercultural Arts, as they were then.
It was in an area in London where there had been a number
of racist murders. That location was very divided in terms of
race and Pan were invited, by a very desperate councillor from
that borough, to go in, do some arts and 'solve' the situation.
Rather than try to get people together from those different
communities, from different physical geographical parts of the
community, I chose to work in very closed groups. I worked
in seven different youth clubs over a summer and they were all
racially and/or gender distinct – Bengali boys, white children
aged eight to ten. I didn't ask for them to be a group of
Bengali boys or white children, they was just who was in that
youth club. It was important for them that they had moments
of being together, sharing experience, working stuff out,
challenging each other, in a space where they were the same as
each other. It almost felt counter-intuitive sometimes because
the whole project was about trying to challenge racism and
prejudice about difference. But they needed to be together

for a bit with people who they recognised as being like them. And then the day came when those seven groups performed to each other – it was a struggle even getting them in the same room – but the fact that they were in the same room at the same time, respectfully watching each other's work, was a really significant moment for those young people, for some of those youth workers and for me. It was an acknowledgement that, however different they might be from one another, they have been through a similar process. They had something in common. Some of those young people decided to get together again and they made another mini community and developed a video project.

So, going back to what all this has taught me about performance, there's something vital about the convention and the ritual of performing, the respect that it takes to watch live performance. You are directing your senses towards a performance, those performers are directing their senses back to

FIGURE 6 *Mojisola Adebayo and Mamela Nyamza in* I Stand Corrected. *Photo: Taryn Burger.*

you. There is a connection between us through that artwork that is, on a good day, memorable. And memories change us: memories feed our imaginations and imagination feeds our sense of what's possible in the world. When we see what's possible in the world we can assess our options and maybe make some change. It's important to be in community, it's important to perform.

4

Lawnmowers Independent Theatre Company: The politics of making

Ali Campbell

Introduction

There are more than 1.2 million adults with learning disabilities in England and they are one of the largest marginalised groups in our society. Issues of choice, inclusion and self-direction are crucial to the everyday wellbeing and human rights of this substantial social group. The last two decades have seen a growing concern about the degree to which professionals have control over their lives: a power not necessarily tempered by real understanding of learning disabled needs. This notably prompted a Government White Paper, *Valuing People: A New Strategy for Learning Disability in the 21st Century* (2001), that sought to advocate the rights of learning disabled people and to propose real and lasting policy change around all aspects of their lives.[1]

The Lawnmowers Independent Theatre Company was founded by Geraldine Ling and Katherine Zeserson in 1986, inspired by their training in Dorothy Heathcote's educational drama work and Augusto Boal's Forum and Image Theatre techniques. The result, over more than twenty years, is a rich synthesis, bringing a formidable array of participatory theatre techniques to bear on the challenges of learning disabled self-determination, advocacy and activism in wider civic society. Lawnmowers are now recognised internationally as a pioneering theatre for social change organisation. All of Lawnmowers' work is rooted in learning disabled experience and articulated through the language of performance, within the broader context of social justice.

The range of the company's work is both prolific and eclectic. Each year, Lawnmowers Independent Theatre Company creates a new co-researched and devised play which tours nationally. These productions and supporting workshops are shaped by the company's signature edgy humour, sharp political insight and participatory ethos. *Walk the Walk* (a response to the Government White Paper, *Valuing People*) features Marlene Dietrich, Dusty Springfield and Elvis in an irreverent critique of the paper's aspiration to afford people with learning disabilities 'the same chance as anyone else to lead a full and interesting life'. *Heroic Feets: A Show about Planning your Life* (2008) offers an eccentric take on how to get and manage a personal budget, a response to recent government legislation *Putting People First*, which directs state funding to individuals to choose the support services that they want. (Prior to this the Local Government Authority decided how money was spent.) This show has a serious intention but is anything but dry or earnest, featuring

---

[1]Department of Health (2001), *Valuing People: A New Strategy for Learning Disability for the 21st Century* (White Paper).

an array of comic book heroes – Batman, Robin, Catwoman, Wonder Woman, Spiderman and The Joker – all assisting in the matter.

Lawnmowers run night clubs, supported and programmed by learning disabled adults in every aspect from marketing to stand-up, DJ-ing to dance classes. They teach and learn continuously in a reciprocal rhythm throughout the year, with commedia, capoeira and carnival artists and makers coming through their doors – no professional standard is compromised. A learning disabled take on these ever-evolving forms goes back out into the world translated, made-over, subverted and adapted for the widening audience of learning disabled people eager for training, empowerment and a chance to find and release their many voices.

In parallel and in dialogue with this continuous performance-making, Lawnmowers deliver a prolific programme of workshops clustered around themes of oppression and empowerment and have developed collaborative partnership work with universities, trade unions and learning disabled groups across the UK and internationally.[2]

This sharing of experience and skills, a prodigious collective act of capacity-building, is only partly explicable by the founding director, Geraldine Ling, and her legendary tenacity and drive. Lawnmowers have gone close to the wall financially many times but continue to reflect, adapt and grow. One of the principles of Lawnmowers' practice that in some way accounts for this ability not only to survive but to thrive is that they train and re-train: themselves and all comers. Each year, they open up to new groups of participants, both learning disabled and those who hope to work with and learn alongside them. This practice provokes many questions

---

[2] A small selection of networks and partners developed through the Lawnmowers Quiet Revolution Programme include the Centre of Excellence and Teacher Training, University of Northumbria; School of Law, University of Northumbria; Manchester University; Crown Prosecution Service; Cumbria University; and Cultural Warriors with People's Palace Projects.

FIGURE 7 Boomba Down The Tyne, *Humsaugh Village Hall, Northerhumberland (31 August 2012). Photograph: Darren Eddon, Available Light Photography.*

about collaboration, education and the politics of community making and belonging that inform this chapter.

For over 20 years, I have worked with this prolific, resilient and ground-breaking company as dramaturg, trainer, mentor and in a range of negotiated roles and guises, always in response to the evolving needs of the core company at any given time. Together we have co-created workshops, films, installations, music and training programmes. I am who I am because I have been *shown* who I am in relationship with Lawnmowers: a reciprocal, iterative relationship, always in flux, always open to question, to risk, to epiphany.

This chapter affords me the opportunity to reflect with multiple perspectives on two decades' personal experience of working with Lawnmowers. Throughout, I select and frame certain moments of meeting, making and performing from an abundance of choice to give access to Lawnmowers' politics and practice. In considering their work, I realised that I am, in effect, reflecting on their influence on my own professional practice, as an artist and scholar, learning/teaching how to meet, make, perform and to do these things self-reflexively. In this chapter, I will tell the story of Lawnmowers from this perspective of shared history, using the technique of Frame Throwing to explore questions of performance and community: to consider what its daily detail can tell us about the character of this small arts organisation and how it has built resilience and strategies for survival. Frame Throwing takes its title from the botanical practice of studying, in depth and detail, a section of a much larger ecosystem and extrapolating from one framed section the rich data against which larger hypotheses can be tested. The positioning of the Frame is not about answering the research question but evidencing it in the unique way that performance practice can.

Frame one: Graeme's house

How does an organisation of this sophistication and productivity operate on a weekly basis with sustained learning disabled ownership at its heart?

In September 2011, I am in Newcastle to run, with Geraldine Ling, an intensive induction for six young trainees to the Lawnmowers. During this visit, I meet Graeme.

Graeme is one of the newest members of the company, having joined through the open recruitment programme. He has already begun a group of his own and is immersed in the can-do of daily workshops and the panoply of the whole operation he has been exposed to, from drop-in to clubs to membership: an open model of empowerment with many potential pathways towards full participation well beyond his original interest in performance for its own sake, much as he still loves that. Graeme has learned how to structure and roll out his creative skills on the job at the same time as absorbing these for himself as a trainee practitioner.

He has said he will take me through the whole current Lawnmower operation with all the daily activities organised as a diagram he has co-devised with other members for professional presentations at conferences to funders, researchers and partners such as universities.

The diagram is of a house: bright orange, full of detail, with many rooms. It aims to capture the how of the company's output in a typical week so that I can attach this to my own exploration of how Lawnmowers operate. It does so neatly, framing these questions as a where.

Graeme is a confident, proud young guide.

The house is a week 'wide'. Some groups (shown as rooms) are open door and subsequently lead further in to the house (to closed/more committed work) or back out to places like Ashington, where Graeme, who is an independent traveller, has taken open mic and clubbing to a new audience well outside of Newcastle. He has come in, been welcomed, skilled up, and now takes away what matters to him. And he keeps coming back. My many questions about the true source of Lawnmowers' productivity, capacity building and sustainability and what it might teach the wider world are answered. Here is Graeme's guide, voiced by him as a formal inventory to what is generated, run, maintained and administered out of that orange house (Swinburne House, Gateshead) in that single week:

- Krokodile Krew (clubbing, DJ-ing, open mic)
- Boi Bumba (cultural collaboration with Brazil; touring)
- School for Fools (mask; clowning; commedia)
- Theatre for Change
- Find Your Voice (North East Warriors Collective/NEWC)
- Beat This (large drumming group)
- Rhumba Palace (music resource/workshop space)

- *Monday club (open-door drop-in/drama)*
- *Focus Group (acting)*
- *Leaping Lawnies (dance)*
- *Sing-sationals*
- *Love Drama*
- *Office*

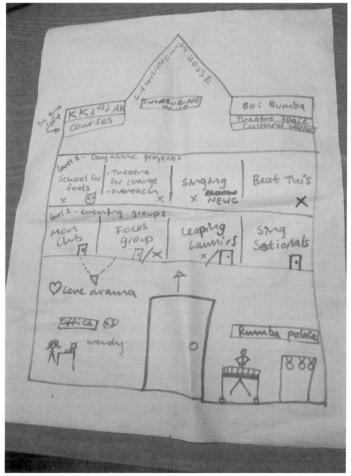

FIGURE 8 *Graeme's House. Photo by Lawnmowers.*

Graeme isn't delivering a lecture on capacity, social capital or sustainability. He is simply showing me how, without the lived and tested experience to lend them depth and weight, these remain (at best) aspirational concepts or (at worst) just the latest glossary of buzzwords being deployed by the same government who are cutting the benefits of tens of thousands like him. As I listen to him and digest the implications of Lawnmowers' model, I understand more deeply how it is rooted in a weekly reality that places true value on all participants and translates that into measurable social action.

As with all cycles of enquiry driven by creative practice itself I am left with fresh and further questions, leading me deeper into the company I like to think I know quite well.

Who are Lawnmowers?

Inevitably, my first questions lead back to the genesis of the company in a confluence between learning disabled culture and both Dorothy Heathcote and Augusto Boal's practices (such as the former's Mantle of the Expert) of working with and through drama, developing exercises to build up the non-professional performer as both author and agent: an expert in their own experience. Both approaches empower the participant with increasing awareness not just to act out the issues and challenges they face but to do so with increasing reflexive awareness: what Friere terms *conscientização*. Through this, the expert becomes active in distilling personal experience into political expertise. Both Boal and Heathcote propose a theatre where a more inclusive, just society is envisaged, modelled, debated and in effect rehearsed. This is the DNA of Lawnmowers' project – a political and educational theatre where traditions of making, training and outreach embody a fertile legacy distilled from the best of twentieth-century applied performance, to the continuing enrichment of community arts practices in the twenty-first.

From my very first devising adventures with Lawnmowers I realised that a headlong dive into the deep end was the only way. It was the mid-eighties and I had been talking to Geraldine for some time about how to reconcile our ongoing reservations about how and when to choose to work with Boal's Forum Theatre with learning disabled *spect-actors* (the active spectators in Boal's participatory methodology).

I had been both empowered and radicalised by my own introduction to Boal's Theatre of the Oppressed using Forum and Image theatre as part of an AIDS education programme with actors and health workers at the National Theatre of Kampala, Uganda in 1990. I then met Geraldine Ling and Katharine Zeserson at the first European Festival of the Theatre of the Oppressed in Massy, south of Paris, in 1991. There was considerable debate amongst the theatre makers present as to whether or not Forum is always the right method to use in our anti-oppression work. I was instantly drawn to Geraldine and Katherine, who were busy hybridising the actor-in-role work of Dorothy Heathcote with their own strong voice practices. They were also running a large women's performance project called Women May and were looking for ways to open up the image-making exercises, fundamental to Boal's highly accessible, democratised dramaturgy, to wider application in communities across the north east of England.

Lawnmowers had begun *in media res*: Geraldine had been scoping in Newcastle and Gateshead for new groups to open up performance workshops to and had found herself one day in a light industrial unit which offered very basic activities to learning disabled people. Almost in passing the person she had come to chat with mentioned that there was a group of people who were always larking about to the radio and cheering everyone up. The five – June Keenlyside, Paul King, Nick Heron, Sharon Harrison and Andy Stafford – became the original Lawnmowers and continued to work with the company. Andy and Paul (until his death in 2013) mentored each new wave of trainees finding their own way into the company's flourishing portfolio of activities. Lawnmowers were, literally, waiting for Geraldine. The role work from Dorothy Heathcote (which Geraldine talks about later in this chapter); their love of music; the natural performativity you meet in a group of like-minded people who keep each other going: Lawnmowers already had their roots in a learning disabled culture forged by necessity, transmitted by story and improvisation like many folk and underground traditions, rich in resilience and waiting for non-learning disabled people to fall into ... or overlook. Geraldine recognised this. The newly formed group decided on its name after a line in a Genesis song, 'I Know What I Like', they all found so funny: 'Me? I'm just a Lawnmower. You can tell me by the way I walk ...'

Forum can expose and address underlying societal and structural oppressions. However, many key questions about its applicability resonate for me still as I reflect on Lawnmowers today.

Frame two: Open wide (1992)

How does a practitioner avoid the trap of performing 'models' (the short scenes in a Forum that the audience must enter and transform through improvisation) that only reinforce the narrative of the learning disabled protagonist as failing, weak and needing rescue? What is the necessary adaptation required so as to overturn the image of learning disabled victimhood?

These questions have fuelled over two decades of collaboration: a quest to find the necessary practical adaptations to Forum to address concrete challenges such as accessibility.

I want to unpack – by throwing a Frame around a moment in rehearsal – an image which epitomises Lawnmowers' evolving devising processes. This moment was from a time long before I had settled into a dramaturgical role with the company and a yearly rhythm where I would follow the indomitable Frances Rifkin, who worked up scenarios from a vast amount of researched material gathered by the group.

This lengthy research period, learning disabled led, still speaks to me of what 'issue-based' theatre of the period so often pre-empted (and thereby missed) by pre-deciding the theme or content of a piece and so undermining a truly learning disabled approach to its articulation and embodiment.

The company at this point inhabited one floor of a large, neglected space in the long-since-developed town centre. I arrived all geared up to go through my best devising exercises, to see the kind of basic scenes the group already had and try to divine what questions were embedded in each one and whether/how role play, Forum or some kind of workshop format would be the best way for Lawnmowers to open these up to other learning disabled audiences for participation. Behind all of these questions (and in the margins of my far too many notebooks) lurked my fear of setting up something patronising or falling into what I still saw as the potential trap of Forum if it were inappropriately chosen or conducted: a reinforcing of the powerlessness of the Protagonist with the *spect-actors* indulging in a game of 'let's pretend'. Augusto would shout out 'Stop! That's magic!' when a fanciful or escapist intervention was made in a regular Forum session and, in my fearfulness and inexperience, I was worried that we would only show scenes that would lead not to empowering solutions but merely invite a hollow tit-for-tat game of Get The Baddie.

We are looking at the issue of how adult learning disabled people are routinely spoken to as children by health profes-sionals, or spoken about as if they aren't there. We have rejected one scene where two well-meaning parents speak over Paul's head as a bit too obvious ('Yes he's been fine mostly doctor, but he does have trouble with his knees, doesn't he Dad?' 'Yes, Mum, that's right. That and his number twos …'). It's funny, but not edgy enough, and if it is to be a model for Forum, it needs to ratchet up the subtle oppressions gradually so that an audience feel increas-ingly impelled to intervene, challenging the progressive undermining of so many learning disabled people implicit in even the most genteel, everyday situations.

Nick offers a recent visit to the dentist. Sharon leaps at the chance to be a dentist: she has a keen eye for caricature based on observation of the many authority figures whose actions, often unconsciously, merely perpetuate a bleakly immutable status quo. The scene has been tried a couple of times before, and as with the doctor scenario features parents, both talking for (and over) Nick in a way that is actually very lightweight compared with his current, very depressing living circumstances.

The dentist appears. Sharon is in her element ... and a large white lab coat.

'NEXT!' (All Sharon's medical scenes start like this. You can't beat it for realism, frankly.) Nick and his parents meekly enter the surgery.

The scene needs a hook. Nick needs to show he is getting increasingly frustrated with his parents' telling the dentist about his teeth. He first looks from one to the other ('Oh, yes, he brushes most regular-ilarily'), then tries to get a word in. We need to up the ante so that the prospective audience of spect-actors can see the chances of his standing up for himself are narrowing down to a point of near impossibility. The scene must follow this trajectory if the meta-intention of provoking as many interventions as possible is to be served, but if everything becomes too impossible too soon we will be just sitting in a shared horror of dentists, now brilliantly reinforced in the audience's minds forever.

Nick is manoeuvered into the dentist's chair. Some of us are laughing, some of us already think it's too late for him to advocate for himself. That's fine, as we need the feeling of possibility/impossibility to see-saw like this if we are to refine the moment into a working Forum that can go on the road and provoke advocacy as a set of realistic interventions by protagonists we haven't met yet. But surely, when he's been talked over, cajoled and manhandled into the chair, it's too late?

'Excuse me,' Nick finally says (lying down). 'I've got something to say too.'

Sharon the dentist, who has already decided with his parents what is wrong, which tooth it is and what to do about it, is taken aback, drill in hand: 'I'm sorry?'

'Well it's just that what's actually wrong is...'

'OPEN WIDE!'

Too late. She's got her hand halfway down his throat. His legs flail in the air. His parents look on, approvingly. He says: 'Euuuuuurgh!'

I can extrapolate so much from this Frame, not least the journey of my own induction into Lawnmowers' method; the deadly accuracy of humour as a cutting and exposing tool; the subversiveness of their portrayal of authority figures; their appropriation of the more Guignol elements of Monty Python and the direct cut to the true power issue at the end of the scene.

What has unfolded is a making over of the sometimes formulaic requirements of Forum (that it show a model of 'failure'; that the protagonist has to be replaced in a realistic intervention) on terms, with the rough texture of humour and within the very robust structure that the devising from actuality has already lent to the scene. Theatrically, there is a magnificent punchline: at the very moment the dentist notices that Nick might have something to say and wavers as she wonders dimly what that might be, her deeply ingrained professional determination to 'fix' him literally takes over her hand (the one holding the drill) and puts it in his mouth. The scene is horribly funny: Nick keeps up the *Euuuuuurgh* for an impressive length of time (legs thrashing) and yet as he does so the joke on the dentist becomes increasingly clear: in a sense that is deeper than this one moment, she and her profession truly don't know what they are doing with learning disabled people, ill served as they are by a training and a system that leaves their habituated, institutionalised actions undoing whatever more compassionate impulse Nick's voice might have aroused.

So the scene works as theatre and at the same time the real issue about the appropriateness of Forum has been resolved. First time round our audience (many of whom will never have seen live performance before) will be hugely, side-splittingly entertained but as we re-wind the scene we will be able to open it up to their enquiry, to possible stopping points where something else might be said, or done, or tried, to make possible a Forum. It will be subtle, complex, nuanced; emotionally and politically intelligent.

A new question arises from this insight: How does embodied knowledge, revealed by Lawnmowers' improvisational and devising practices, apply to the most telling questions of power and powerlessness as experienced by learning disabled adults in daily life? Does this humour have an impact beyond the temporary release of satire?

Frame three:
Billy and The Big Yin (2005)

I bring to this question a Frame from the middle of a devising process that took me to a place well outside my comfort zone to expose an 'issue' in a way I would simply never have attempted alone as a dramaturg. I want to show that there have been moments that my own unconscious retention of the basic control over the point-of-view and consequently both the style and essential power politics of a piece of work has been exposed: lovingly, humourously, shockingly, irreversibly.

Invariably in exercises, name games and full-scale drama work the learning disabled adults I have worked with use the performance space to inhabit high status roles. These are always appropriated with irony and wit and made over to voice transgressive and often anarchic points of view – June as Marlene Dietrich, Sharon as Dusty Springfield, Paul as

Elvis – showing me something very much more canny and subversive than the awful doomed escapism of mainstream talent shows.

Andy's hero is Billy Connolly. *Billy and the Big Yin* (2005) is a kind of biopic, with Andy as Billy, the best-loved Glaswegian of all. Through Lawnmowers' process, the life of the man we know as The Big Yin is a revelation. We are working from his wife Pamela Stephenson's biography of him, which has outraged some quarters of Scottish society (and beyond) with its frank disclosures of childhood abuse, the incompetence of institutions supposedly there to help and, tellingly, Connolly's own moderate learning difficulties, with which Andy identifies. Andy Stafford himself, in the years I have known him, has become a key Lawnmowers' worker, gained his driving licence and passed his computing exams and, in truth, might not be diagnosed or statemented today as he was as a child. So who labels whom, who statements whom, and who might reclaim that language and forge a new, empowered, self-defining one are themes just asking to be mined by the choice of Andy, the actor of *Billy and The Big Yin*, before we even start.

Mistakenly, I think this process is going to be what the real Billy would call a 'doddle', as the connections between his life and a broader message of empowerment, Lawnmowers style, seem more than usually clear. We will be shocking! He will be laughed at but will win in the end! Then the nuns appear …

How are we going to show that Billy was betrayed by institutions? This is my question for today's rehearsal and I have no idea how we will approach it.

I ask June and Sharon to pick a moment where the original story really says how it is to be outnumbered, shrunken, blamed and diminished just for being. June chooses the 'bit with the nuns'. I don't even remember nuns from the book and I've certainly skirted around the question of whether we are going to have Sisters in this show, but oh boy, here they are, showing what Catholicism did for Billy.

Take One: Billy on floor. Enter nuns.

June and Sharon have dispensed with dialogue. Each has managed to fashion a wimple from the dressing up box and crucifixes have been improvised from something culinary close to hand. Andy hasn't been particularly warned that this section of his hero's life is up next. No problem: no dialogue. Instead the nuns skip gaily around him as he shrinks into an ever-smaller ball. They are singing: 'How do you solve a problem like Maria?' ... and hitting him with home-made crucifixes.

A pause. Some of us are literally on the floor. As dramaturg, I try to pull myself together. Maybe we need a line just to explain, possibly, why they are being so mean to him? I've been laughing too much to manage more than this feeble suggestion but I'm scared too. The nuns are scary and how some of our audiences might receive this is even scarier (June, for example, lives in a Catholic-run home, and so do many of our audiences).

Just a line to help the audience ... understand, maybe?

June agrees (but I can tell she's just humouring me).

Take Two: Billy on floor. Enter nuns. They skip gaily around him as he shrinks into an ever-smaller ball, singing 'How do you solve a problem like Maria?' (reprise).

The nuns start hitting him with home-made crucifixes:

'YOU WANNA KNOW WHY WE'RE DOING THIS, EH? WELL, JESUS IS DEAD, AND IT'S ALL [thwack] YOUR [thwack] FAULT!'

The scene, once the shock wears off, works. The grotesques remind me, again, of Monty Python with 2000 years' misinterpretation of Gospel so brilliantly distilled into one line that there is a perfectly judged distancing device at work. The focus is on Billy as he shrinks under the verbal and physical blows, not letting us off the hook with a cheap laugh but forcing us to look at the scene through the eyes of a disturbed, abused but (we now know) gifted, undefeatable child. People will complain. But it gives us the chance to craft a scene around a moment that will allow an audience to use it to look at their own experience of institutional bullying with the all-important distancing device firmly in place.

And that's how a culture of improvisation can be brought to a genuine critique of monolithic subject matter. That was almost fifteen years ago at the time of writing and its legacy is something I still carry gratefully into every rehearsal.

Frame four: Lawnmowers in the hotseat (2011)

How has what I have called the DNA of Lawnmowers' devising methods continued to be so generative over the last two decades?

In September 2011 – within a performative session designed to research this chapter – Geraldine Ling and I are reflecting on the lived history of Lawnmowers with a new cohort of trainee facilitators, mostly recent graduates from community arts and music courses locally. We are taking it in turns to hotseat one another and to relate personal narrative to a larger discourse.

It is my turn to hotseat Geraldine. I ask her about the sources, the tributaries, which shape Lawnmowers today.

Geraldine: I was working with Dorothy Heathcote and Katherine Zeserson doing projects across the whole community. We were doing a lot of women and girls' work in role. People were put in a role such as the scientist in the drama. Once you have taken on a role, it means you feel differently about yourself. People with learning disabilities

*have further to jump really in terms of not being expected
to be experts. A lot of it was what Dorothy called 'a shift
in the head'. Of course you've not been factory workers in
the fish factory for twenty-five years, but you can imagine
what it's like. Stepping into the drama, then stopping and
analysing your place in it ... What is all this about? Who is
responsible? What are the things we can look at? It was the
stopping and starting that was quite new to me: I thought
you just got a drama under way, but in this method you
reflect. For example, Lawnmowers became experts on HIV
...*

*Geraldine has reminded me of an emergent moment, a
frame-within-a-frame, from 1997 ...*

Frame five: Devising The Big Sex Show (1997)

How have Lawnmowers maintained a learning disabled led
and held space that enables their project to go beyond arts-
based work into activism, training and advocacy?

*I am still pretty new to Lawnmowers but I have been
embraced by their rhythm of shaping each new show with
a particular eye to how its participatory elements will
work and which of the scenes, already peer-researched
and worked up as improvisations, will lend themselves
to Forum. But* The Big Sex Show? *Deep down in me a
negativity lurks, born of a lifetime's subliminal conditioning about how to see and deal with learning disabled
adults: as children.*

*Paul, June, Sharon, Andy and Nick are constructing a
waiting room and a doctor's surgery around me.*

*I look into myself, trying to enquire of myself where
this odd stuck-ness is coming from and there it is. Even
if (unavoidably) the tumescent subject of sex might arise,*

learning disabled adults (surely?) DO NOT HAVE SEX. *At the very bottom of this disempowering conditioning (and my discomfort alerts me to its toxicity) are the very real ideological forces that shaped it, eugenics among them. They lead to the sterilising room and other more dreadful chambers behind that one: spaces in the twentieth century that turned it, for so many, into Hell.*

Paul and Sharon work out what they are going to do.

Too much analysis – I am worried that this time I won't be able to deal with what Lawnmowers have asked me to do.

June puts her white coat on.

I bottle up my fears. Andy Stafford beams at me. 'Are you ready?' is the meaning of that confident smile of his. I'll fake it to make it. 'Yes,' I lie.

The improvisation begins …

The Big Sex Show has a cabaret format, aiming to animate real-life, peer-researched incidences where sex and sexuality are explored through participatory performance.

Paul and June have created an improvisation out of their own recent visit to the local family planning clinic, which welcomes sexually active learning disabled couples.

Andy plays the receptionist; Paul and Sharon (a real-life couple) … a real-life couple. June is reprising one of her favourite authority figure roles: the Well-Intentioned Lady Doctor.

PAUL AND SHARON ENTER THE BROOK ADVISORY CLINIC

RECEPTIONIST *(poshly): Kinnayhelpyew?*

SHARON: Yes, we're here to see the doctor about birth control.

RECEPTIONIST: *Thet's ebsolutely fayne. Pleeze beseetit.*

[PAUSE]

SHARON: I'm a bit nervous, are you?

PAUL: Aye, I am that.

RECEPTIONIST: NEXT!

JUNE: (Advancing with stethoscope, smiling)

Good after-noooon!

PAUL: We're engaged and we've decided we don't want children yet but we're having sex, like, and she doesn't want to go on the pill.

JUNE: That's fine. In that case I would suggest using a condom. Have either of you used one before?

SHARON: (Embarrassed): No.

JUNE: Well that's not a problem because I have a man's penis here in my cupboard. All you have to do is roll a condom on, and then after you've finished you can tie it in a knot, throw it in the bin or burn it. Is that clear?

DRAMATURG: CUT!

There are times when you know what nearly dying with laughter actually means. All apprehensiveness about whether we are going to make a memorable scene vanishes. June fishes out the plaster model penis in question to explain, but it's far too late. You know that line in a play, the one you keep getting wrong so you go back over and over in rehearsals, until the mistake has been better rehearsed – and is now more fully entrenched – than any other moment in the play? This is such a moment. I will remember it all of my life with joy and gratitude. I can see that June doesn't mind the hysterics. The show is going to tour with the strong probability of a severed organ's appearance from June's cupboard now as intrinsic to its health education message as an invisible dagger to the Scottish Play.

My nerves have gone. I've tears on my cheeks. We might need to take some of the volunteers at the day centre aside now and then just to prepare them for the show's adult content ... I make a note.

We can do anything, we Lawnmowers. And that, I realise, with a jolt, in 1997 and 2011, one space fourteen years apart, is what Lawnmowers have always taught me.

On that day I *knew* the Forum would be fine: Paul and June had researched the scene, they owned both that scene and the means to enter, adjust or change it by participation. Their rules. If, during the Forum, learning disabled *spect-actors* corrected the doctor, questioned the doctor, argued with the doctor or even fled the doctor, Forum would still work. It is – by Boal's earliest definitions – a game.

Back to frame four (2011)

Geraldine's hotseating continues. She continues the story of The Big Sex Show *to include its enormously influential international touring.*

Geraldine: [...] Lawnmowers became experts on HIV. We made loads of plaster of Paris penises because we had to use them in all the workshops that we ran, so that people could put condoms on them. The show we took to Poland was televised on national TV. Someone broke the penis. June was called by the Catholic-run home she lived in at the time to ask how it had gone, and she said: 'Well, it all went fine. The penis I normally use got broken, so we just borrowed a vibrator.'

Ali: There is always this point with Lawnmowers where total comedy, pure accident, genuine expertise and lots of empowerment – this rich, chaotic mixture – are all happening at the same time, and then an institution goes: 'Wait a minute. This is too messy/funny/sexy. This is not the illustrated lecture we expected. The play is supposed to illustrate a message, and the message is one we have already decided is good for learning disabled people.' How do Lawnmowers depart from that?

Geraldine: They research everything for a long time before rehearsals even begin. There is always a sense that no matter where we start there are always workshops, and they are more important than the show, although the shows are classics that are remembered by all who see them. But Lawnmowers would always workshop with other learning disabled participants. That was crucial: everything was built up from that. And of course we had all sorts of amazing people coming in to Lawnmowers: new and younger people bringing in ideas. We have built up the work from that and it has always been learning disabled led. We've learned how to do things in a slightly odd way. People come in and although this approach is not conventional it is to learning disabled people's lives: it's all within that spirit.

Frame six: Here and now

These Frames, placed over specific moments in more than twenty years of collaboration, reveal so much about what a mutually pedagogical relationship can be. In that time, I have had relationships with many other companies who have gone to the wall: theatre in education groups whose grant support eventually ran out, too often as a consequence of their own energies doing the same; education departments of major producing houses and museums who moved on from what they perceived as single-issue projects in pursuit of funding streams attached to ever-shifting notion of outreach and inclusion.

And so back to 2011: crossing the Tyne by its oldest bridge and looking along the glittering water to the newest one, Newcastle and Gateshead's recently transformed river-scape is a story, told by a series of architectural interventions, about post-industrial life in the twenty-first century. Along from the contemporary arts temple of the Baltic, high up the river bank from the shining promise of the Sage, housed in Swinburne House (the old Gateshead Public Library), Lawnmowers have been walking the talk of outreach and social inclusion since quite some time before such aspirations were enshrined in the mission statements (and funding agreements) that have made such undeniably beautiful public spaces possible.

Recent discourse in the north east on this theme began with Antony Gormley's epic statue, the Angel of the North: lots of municipal talk about things iconic; their benefits to tourism; their referencing and celebration of a lost industrial past and the potential for an alchemical arts-based re-emergence as new industries for a new century. I enter the library, looking back at the Sage and the Baltic. I wonder about this doctrine – that the Arts can initiate 'regeneration' – and find myself asking, here, now, today: How can we extrapolate an approach from Lawnmowers' daily working practices that re-claims the undisputed role of participatory arts-based work as a grass-roots movement, complete with its own alternative pedagogy and micro-economy?

In 2005, Lawnmowers commissioned Lodestar to carry out an analysis of the social return on investment (SROI) of the company's work. This report evidences the social value of the work, placing an economic value on it, and therefore providing a way of articulating the impact of the work in an evaluative culture. Whilst a SROI analysis may be considered to translate and reduce the live-ness of the work and individuals' experiences within it into pounds and pence, this articulation allows us insight into how an organisation like Lawnmowers is expected to adapt and articulate its worth to different audiences. The following section outlines an area of the report reflecting on June's experience. As we have seen in the previous frames, June is an actor of considerable resource, expertise and improvisational power. But in the SROI report, she is also the story of Lawnmowers, of what is possible within a small client-led organisation for both the individual and for society.

June is a founder member of Lawnmowers. Previously she had attended an adult training centre five days a week and done contract work counting out plastic bin-liners or stamping prescription pads. She had left school with no qualifications and was not linked in to any further education. She travelled very little and lived at home where there were very few opportunities to socialise. She had very few friends.

When Lawnmowers were established time was spent on devising the touring work and undertaking all the training that was required to produce and tour. June has devised and toured over a dozen national shows and is particularly known for her work on *The Big Sex Show*, *Lawnmowers Strike Back* and *Walk the Walk*. Following this her training with Lawnmowers led to qualifications accredited by Tyneside Open College and recognised by The Arts Council and the National Disability Arts Forum. The training included basic computing, financial management, office administration and fundraising, creative arts skills at an intermediate level and performance techniques, including devising a show, technical aspects of theatre, planning organising and editing a video. Now June is part of a vibrant team and she is far more socially active: she has a range of friends through her contact with Lawnmowers.

Since becoming a Lawnmower June has been the co-presenter for the BBC *Go For It* programme ... Her work experience includes the following theatre residencies: North West Disability Arts; Prism (Cumbria); Carousel (Brighton); Wales; Fraserborough and Galway. She has worked nationally including tours of Ireland and Scotland and internationally in Poland, Canada and Spain.[3]

Bearing in mind that over the past two decades June has trained hundreds in participatory arts techniques and her work as a performer has been seen by thousands, we can begin to extrapolate the capacity of Lawnmowers for social change. However, recent governments have responded by cutting even the kind of work, counting bin-liners, that she began with; necessitating a translation of this creative output into the kind of economic data required by career politicians. The report frames the financial impact of Lawnmowers in the following way:

Total direct expenditure on Lawnmowers (accounts at July 2005): £263,000.

End Value created by Lawnmowers Independent Theatre Co: £1,381,741 after 5 years.

Added value of project (End Value less initial investment) = £1,118,741.

SROI ratio (arrived at by calculating the gains, subtracting the costs and dividing the end result by the costs) = 1: 4.25.

That is to say that for each pound invested in Lawnmowers, the project returns £4.25 to the economy.

---

[3]Karl Leathem, *Lawnmowers Independent Theatre Company, Theatre for Change: A Social Return on Investment Report.* Lodestar, 2006.

In this case the payback is over a remarkable period of less than a year. That is to say that the staff and members directly involved in the delivery of Lawnmowers' programme between them return the value of the investment made in them by the funders of the project in a very short period indeed: nine months. In accounting convention such a payback would be considered a highly attractive investment.

Conclusion

Throughout this chapter, I have selected and framed certain moments of meeting, making and performing to give the reader access to Lawnmowers' politics and practice. In considering their work I have realised that I am also, in effect, reflecting on their influence on my professional practice, as

FIGURE 9 *Ali Campbell and Paul King in a Lawnmowers' workshop. Photograph by the Lawnmowers.*

an artist and scholar, learning/teaching how to meet, make, perform and to do these things self-reflexively. As I have shown, the positioning of the Frame is not about 'answering' the research question, but evidencing it in the unique way that performance practice can. As a group often talked about rather than consulted, Lawnmowers have by their power-fully inclusive ethos and through their transformative creative practices been one of the biggest influences on my own thirty years as an artist, activist and educator. So it follows in the interest of equality and transparency – of solidarity with Lawnmowers – that I have to put myself inside the Frame. I need to ask a question, of and for myself: what is it to be in the Lawnmowers? Can non-learning disabled people 'belong' to them?

Frame seven: A welcome to lawnmowers

September 2011. Lawnmowers' Training.

Geraldine's welcome ripples out through the morning. I meet the young trainees, all of whom are already working alongside one of Lawnmowers' projects and – in the case of the musicians – have actually initiated and shaped these themselves. There is a feeling of capability, of capacity, of readiness. Only a few months since graduation and some of this group seem to have undergone accelerated profes-sional growth.

One exercise, 'How I Got Here', will generate the material for a day-long chorus of personal narratives. Each participant, Geraldine included, will tell the journey they have made as individuals through the old library doors in Gateshead or into the nationwide sprawl of community centres and arts venues where they first fell among Lawnmowers. Boal's Stroboscopic Image will be used to play back: each narrator positioning themselves in a series of freeze frames that represent the witnesses' 'take' on their journey and are viewed in silence, one at a time, by the group who close their eyes in between images to maximise their impact and deepen their fragile quality of shared, negotiated, open-ended meaning. The room fills with images of meeting, making, contact, inclusion and growth.

Each voice is heard describing in detail their first encounter with Lawnmowers: how they were themselves included as an 'able' person; how this is the way they found their own path into a place with the company as intern, graduate trainee or full-timer; how the ethos of empowerment was first imparted to them as an act of generosity and a subversion of a relationship often expected to be uneven, pedagogically and socially; how Lawnmowers' culture of mentorship has in particular spoken to highly idealistic young graduates who have found themselves in a provisional role (often by way of a workshop) with the company and consequently come to realise that are apprentices.

As each shows/tells their story, the ethos of the company, its welcome to all collaborators, is manifested in many different ways.

One of the young trainee facilitators, Josh, reflects on being part of Lawnmowers:

I realise that I come here to receive as well as give. In the singing workshop for example there were lots of moments where I just experienced a great amount of generosity from the people participating. Sometimes it was what we did that gave the opportunity for that, but a lot of the time it was the environment that's here: it's an opening for people to give a huge amount.

One guy had very little speech and was in a wheelchair. There's a lot of fear about how you interact with people with disabilities – what you are allowed to do – so it's very easy for these people to be invisible, for us not to open our eyes. Once, we were doing a song, and I suddenly got a sense of the energy coming from one of the men in the group. He was giving all his being to everyone he interacted with, sharing with everybody. Everyone in the room was getting so much from this person who was not 'leading', not 'teaching' something: he just entered into a space where he had been given an opportunity to express himself in a very open way.

Although there is a lot about building skills that is good and important – skills are a way to develop, to recognise yourself and they give you a currency to go out into the world – they are not the only thing. It's about seeing that everybody is an individual who is a gift to the world, it's about allowing yourself to be who you are, in a space that encourages that.

I realise I have written the word *Philoxenia* on my pad.

The ancient Greek concept of *Philoxenia* celebrates the welcoming space as one where the guest is seen as gift and as such is given the best the house has to offer. Lawnmowers open a space to us where this underpins all their practice, rippling out into the wider world of learning disabled culture, claiming a proud space among oral traditions world-wide where the newest entrant is celebrated.

Never do I enter Lawnmowers' space without the hospitality of laughter and an allowing-ness of 'mistakes' to enfold me. Practised individually, this generosity of spirit is easy to understand: in a life-time of being underrated, marginalised, laughed at and bullied, the learning disabled actor (given a safe theatre space) can turn all of this rich experience of status games (exposing the tactics whereby oppressors maintain the status quo) into what Boal terms an 'arsenal' of transferable techniques for subversion, advocacy, empowerment and activism. The hospitable permission to laugh at oppression makes for a feisty, knowing, quirky kind of performer, well-prepared for haphazard improvisatory strategies to deal with 'mistakes' in rehearsal as well as to rehearse for 'real life'.

But when that individual generosity is compounded, embodied and extended as *philoxenia* – as a lived group ethos – it evidences a set of principles underpinning the Lawnmower's making, training, development, fundraising and everyday operation. Transformative forces are marshalled, capable of taking (say) health provision, including the training of GPs and receptionists, and getting it to take a good look at itself. Not by blaming, but by showing truth from a rarely sought yet invaluable point of view: that of the person on the receiving end of your often haplessly well-intentioned mistakes. Not to be told what you are doing 'wrong' but to be shown with grace, wisdom and plain common sense how things might – if we reconnect with our infinite potential to change – be made so very much better.

* * *

This chapter is dedicated to Paul King, founding member of The Lawnmowers Theatre Company, who died in 2013. A great actor, teacher and friend. You showed us all what a life well lived can be.

5

Bobby Baker

Interview and introduction by Caoimhe McAvinchey

Bobby Baker is a performance artist whose work has garnered international critical and popular acclaim over the past four decades.

After training as a painter at St Martin's School of Art, Baker's early work, including *Meringue Ladies World Tour I & II* (1973) and *Edible Family in a Mobile Home* (1976), defied the limitations of canvas to embrace the possibilities of food and performance. *Drawing On a Mother's Experience* (1988) and the shows within the *Daily Life Series* (1991–2001) offered small, domestic and habitual acts as indicators of wider cultural practices and concerns.

Since the late 1990s work such as *Pull Yourself Together* (2000), *How to Live* (2007) and *Give Peas a Chance* (2008) has more explicitly reflected on Baker's own experiences of mental illness and recovery whilst critiquing the social, economic and cultural impacts of stigma and the pharmacological and health insurance industries that surround it. *Diary Drawings*, an exhibition of Bobby's illustrated account of her mental and physical illness and recovery, was launched at the

Wellcome Collection (2009) and continues to tour venues including psychiatric units, museums and universities. Her book, *Diary Drawings: Mental Illness and Me* (2010), won the MIND book of the year (2011).

Throughout her career Baker has sought to make her work accessible to a wide audience, not just those familiar to or with easy access to the cultural mainstream: *Cook Dems* (1990) toured women's refuges, coffee groups and local businesses, and her recent production *Mad Gyms and Kitchens* (2011) invited a dialogue with audiences across local arts and health networks about strategies for wellbeing.

Baker has a strong relationship with Queen Mary, University of London: she was an AHRC Creative Fellow in the School of English and Drama (2005–2008) and awarded an honorary doctorate in 2011.

* * *

You are currently developing The Daily Life Project, an arts and digital research project with communities across east London. Can you explain more about what it is and how the idea for it evolved?

When I think about how I am as a person, how I work as an artist, I love people: I'm completely fascinated by them and I want to know about their lives. That's where *The Daily Life Project* comes from. It's a three-year exploration of the East End to meet individuals from all walks of life who have personal experience of mental health issues. It's about discovering and promoting people's unacknowledged expertise at developing ingenious strategies for daily living.

At various stages in my work, I've wanted to take work to where people are, where they already come together as a group who don't necessarily see themselves as an art audience. When I do a show about something very personal it's not intended to be confessional: the aim is to be objective. One of things that I like most about doing the work I do is when people see something of themselves through my work and talk about themselves. In the shows that look at a set of activities, like shopping in *How To Shop* (1993), the audiences forget that it's about me and they talk about their own experiences. That has happened with certain shows very strongly. Over the years, I've become more and more interested in thinking about how to extend this dialogue with and between people, how to enable people to make their own work.

I've tried engaging with particular communities in various ways. In the 1990s I became interested in making work based on my own experience of mental illness. I worked with Mark Storor to run a pilot project with people with experience of mental health issues in collaboration with the Studio Upstairs.[1] Although he'd worked on *Grown-up School* (LIFT 1999) with me previously, we'd never worked together in this way before. We did six workshops and produced all sorts of things in a local arts centre and it was fun. But it was a really steep learning curve for me. We could do really great things in three hours but, at times, it felt risky: I didn't know enough about the people, I didn't have enough of a relationship with them. So that sense of wondering how to do that, how to work with people, carried on.

When I came to Queen Mary in 2005 I felt a wonderful sense of arrival at a space, an institution, a community. I loved meeting all these new people – academics, administrators, cleaners – and the geography of things completely enthralled me: the campus is in the East End surrounded by extraordinarily diverse communities. I got involved with social geography, went to seminars and conferences, and it was like the roof of my head lifting off. I realised that that's what I wanted to do – to be a fake social geographer who researches

---

[1] 'Studio Upstairs is a working arts community. It is a place for people to express their talents through the arts who for reasons of mental health difficulties or emotional distress, choose not to participate in traditional arts institutions.' http://www.studioupstairs.org.uk/ (accessed 10 April 2013).

the area. I wanted to do a piece of work where I got to know more about the people on the campus and more about the people who lived nearby. Their lack of personal knowledge of each other fascinated me. How could I bring out some sort of daily experiences so people were not so isolated from one another? How could I support generous relationships with and between people?

In the meantime I developed *Mad Gyms and Kitchens* (2011) involving people with personal experience of mental health issues, like me. I felt more and more, from my personal experience of being on the receiving end of projects, that it was a top-down approach: people within the mental health system were being delivered to rather than having any say in what they wanted or needed.

There is enormous fear, stigma and ignorance around mental illness. The Time to Change campaign has raised a particular kind of statistical awareness – that one in four people will have experience of mental health problems – which means there is a complex diverse community of people who are disconnected from each other. It can affect everyone, not just people in hospitals or day centres: they might be working in corporate organisations or stuck at home with a baby or a seemingly cool young person who's struggling a bit. They might not be part of any official network of support. But despite the success of the campaign, there is still stigma and discrimination.

The words in the diagnostic system for mental illness are a psychiatric medicalising of distress. The process of being diagnosed with mental illness makes you believe you are the problem, right to your very core. If you're going through a really bad time and you have those words applied to you, you embody the problem: you feel really bad but also you can become oppressed by the label of 'depression' or 'anxiety' or of 'being unable to cope'. Those words can stop you moving out from that moment. I wondered, how do people with personal experience of mental health issues come up with ingenious ways of enjoying daily life? How are these strategies

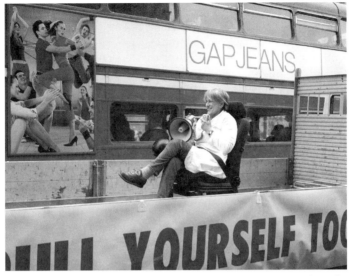

FIGURE 10 *Bobby Baker,* Pull Yourself Together *(2000). Photo by Hugo Glendinning.*

overlooked or underestimated by health professionals, or by people themselves?

The process of being objective and thinking about mental health difficulties is to gradually learn to empower yourself, to regain your autonomy. I want to find a way for people to share their expertise about mental illness and recovery with each other to consider, what it is that makes your life worth living, what it is that you value in yourself, what are your strengths and what could you learn from each other? The Daily Life Project provides a context and structure for collaboration through the arts, for generating new ways of understanding and representing the daily lives of people with personal experience of mental health issues.

In the neighbourhoods of east London, there are established communities of people who know things about mental illness and support people. There are experts by experience and professional experts: I want to develop a sense of that collective knowledge so as to make it more accessible. *The Daily Life Project* is about connecting people, facilitating meeting points and opportunities, real and online, where people can get to know each other – to create a temporary virtual community as a paradigm for how we all live.

The plan is to set up a sort of 'mobile art school' to foster opportunities for people to engage with the arts, and other local people. Commissioned work can be curated on a virtual gallery offering a platform for new work so that other communities of people running arts and health projects across the country and in other parts of the world, can see what we did. This can so easily seem to be, 'let's all be positive and cheerful'. But it isn't that. It's a really thoughtful way of looking at mental illness through creative and digital arts, though collaboration, through recognising our resilience and innate expertise.

Both Mad Gyms and Kitchens *and* The Daily Life Project *strongly engage with ideas of reflecting or developing a community on-line. Can you explain more about how and why the digital has become an integral part of your work?*

Housework House (2008–present) was my first interactive web project. I worked with Deborah May, Sian Stevenson and groups of older people in Notting Hill and Archway to create a gallery of short films of daily life, of people doing housework that they were good at, which were curated on a website. There was an illustration based on my house with twenty-six numbers and you went round the house, clicked on a number and you would see, for example Albert showing how he made an omelette with two half eggs, or the woman who'd come in from walking the dog and use her foot to mop the floor with a towel, or the woman who'd tinkle the piano. It was really simple and really moving. Somehow people heard about it in Australia and the USA, and told me how they loved it and used it – in digital conferences or to make life more bearable. *Housework House* gave me a sense of the capacity of communication with the World Wide Web.

Then I had all these quite serious physical problems and was endlessly recovering from surgery, unable to physically go to things and more and more able to be online. I found out so much. It gives people a capacity to be resourceful, resilient and independent, to connect and be connected.

A major part of The Daily Life Project *is both accessing and developing networks of people who have expertise in mental illness. You are doing this through making connections with local people interested in arts and health and then touring* Mad Gyms and Kitchens *and a small exhibition of the* Diary Drawings. *Can you explain more about* Mad Gyms and Kitchens?

Mad Gyms and Kitchens was part of the London 2012 Unlimited season, which funded disabled artist led work for the Cultural Olympiad. It was one of twenty-nine commissions. The aim, which always influences what you produce, was to do something you'd not had a chance to do before. I wanted to make a show for people who would just come to it with an open mind, in places where people meet locally. I have made large scale work before; *How to Live* (2007) in the Barbican was a massive production with a huge set and seventeen people working on it. It was very successful in its own terms, but I wanted to take a small show with a degree of that sophisticated elegance, with a beautifully crafted set, to people who were not a traditional arts audience. *Mad Gyms and Kitchens* is a small show, just me, a young performer and a stage manager, touring across the country to small venues playing to audiences of sixty to seventy.

I worked with the sculptor Charlie Whittuck, and he came up with the idea of flight cases. They are beautiful boxes that unfold full of colour and props into a gym, a kitchen, a bed and my living room – my 'recovery' apparatus. The final box,

FIGURE 11 *Bobby Baker,* First F.E.A.T. *(2008). Photo: Andrew Whittuck.*

the Art Kart, has tea, biscuits – including bourbons – sugar and high-quality art materials.

My performance lasts about fifty minutes. There's a bit at the beginning where I've got a screen where I've done a drawing of myself that's been blown up: it's a rather gross, naked version of myself, like a medical diagram with a lot of points on it, and I do a bit of a lecture about all the things that have been wrong with me – all the psychiatric diagnoses, all the physical things that got overlooked, like breast cancer and arthritis, and all the operations I've had. And I say, 'So that was then, but look at me now, I'm perfect!' And then I go through the four boxes – talking about myself, my life, really focusing on what I do that makes me feel good. And then, towards the end, there's a sense that I'm a little bit lonely and then I do this ridiculous penguin dance and say to the audience, 'Well, actually it wasn't about me, it's about you – what do you do to feel good?' And everyone is offered a drink and biscuit and art materials. Generally people just can't wait to get their hands on the art materials and draw their top-tips for well-being. These are put up on a wall and everybody chats about them. People tend to hang around for half an hour, sometimes longer. It's very informal, a conversation really. Then some of the illustrations go on a digital scrapbook to document and share with others.[2]

Humour is one of the major characteristics of your work. In Redeeming Features of Everyday Life *you refer to it as 'a valuable method of communication' and 'an effective way of conveying complex and sometimes subversive ideas'.[3] But it's also a very generous act because you use it to reveal something of yourself – that is an invitation for the audience rather than a confession to it. Your work is never just about you, it's always about what your audience think and feel about something.*

The audience is a group of people thinking about things that matter to me: what is family life? What is domestic work? How do you consider the detail of daily life? What do you think about how you label people who are unhappy? It's all of that.

The whole history of the notion of personality disorder is tainted and mired in terrible stigma and abuse. It's comes from the psychiatric, pharmaceutical and health insurance industries. I have a really strong critique of it, along with many others. But it also dogs me because it's in my medical records. In *Mad Gyms and Kitchens*, because I'm talking about having been mentally ill and the labels it is given, there is a risk that that is how I'm referred to. But this risk and some personal sacrifice have been necessary to say, now look, the problems with those labels are that if you say somebody's got

---

[2]'Daily Life Limited, Your Own Top Tips', a digital scrapbook of audiences' suggestions for approaches to 'wending your way to wellness' after *Mad Gyms and Kitchens*, http://dailylifeltd.co.uk/mad-gyms-and-kitchens/gallery/ (accessed 12 April 2013).
[3]Michele Barrett and Bobby Baker (eds), *Bobby Baker: Redeeming Features of Everyday Life* (London and New York: Routledge, 2007), pp. 26, 27.

a disordered personality, it's a trap: you're saying somebody can never *not* be that thing. And you're also very forcefully claiming there is an ordered person. It's semantically flawed to the very core.

But I feel that the risk of doing that, of being open and funny and carrying on, is worth it if it changes the perception of people like me, of people who have had an experience of mental illness, but have good lives and are valued. It's worth it if people recognise their own capacity, their own experience and expertise. It's a very long journey.

I'm very political about the stigmatisation of people with mental health problems – the psychiatric industries, the opportunity for people's lives being better, the need for more knowledge and understanding. I realise that as an artist probably the best, most effective thing I can contribute to this dialogue, to try and tackle the injustice, is to just make work: get on with my life, live what I've learned and have a good time.

6

Meeting the others: Jeremy Weller's Grassmarket Project

Richard Ings

> The stage for me is a kind of laboratory in which all
> humanity can be explored. People ask whether this is a
> social approach but I don't think it is. It's more spiritual
> or psychological. It's about when you're not acting, when
> you're authentic, when you're real. I don't think people on
> my stage mimic and, when you go to my plays, you don't
> have to suspend your disbelief – because what you're
> seeing is real.
> JEREMY WELLER

In 1990 the hottest theatre ticket at the Edinburgh Fringe
Festival was *Glad*, a play about homelessness. The venue
was the Grassmarket, on the site of a local mission helping
out people who lived rough on the city's streets. What
made the production such a huge draw was the innovative
approach its director, Jeremy Weller, was taking to the subject.
Instead of using a cast of professional actors, all but one of

the performers were local homeless people themselves. The drama, as it unfolded, was directly based on their own words: their own life stories that they had shared with the director and his assistants. It made for an unforgettable evening, knowing that what we were seeing was probably as authentic an account of homelessness as could be imagined on stage. *Glad* earned glowing press coverage and a Fringe First award, as did subsequent plays that Weller went on to present in the city over the next few years.

Flash forward a decade and a half, and I am witnessing a roomful of young people being auditioned for a new production, *The Foolish Young Man*. Commissioned by the rejuvenated Roundhouse, the legendary London venue, to launch its studio programme for local young people, this production is, like *Glad*, to feature just one professional actor, David Harewood. He is the eponymous young man and the foil to a crowd of vociferous, much younger people, who take advantage of his impulsive invitation to one of them to camp out in his apartment. The piece that emerges a few months after the audition is by turns painful, hilarious, revelatory, shocking. As in 1990, the stories are the cast's own – anecdotes and confessions shared with the director about their lives on run-down estates and in pupil exclusion units, about their involvement in drug abuse and gangs, about violence and sexual exploitation. I saw this script develop from its beginnings in the often startling personal histories volunteered at the audition, among them a teenager describing how she had found her drug-addicted father lying dead on the kitchen floor and a young Somali man telling us how, a few weeks previously, his teenaged cousin had been stabbed to death over a territorial dispute.

The company led by Jeremy Weller is called the Grassmarket Project, a moniker that nods to its origins in Edinburgh and its first production but which also implies that the last twenty odd years of theatre (and more recently film) can be designated as a 'project'. It is, in fact, possible to see all of Weller's productions as a single body of work, shaped by his determination to force us – the audience – to confront, listen to, understand and engage with those on the margins of mainstream society.

Putting the company into context

The Grassmarket Project aims to achieve a particularly raw kind of authenticity, where people speak their own truths in their own voices. Out of the experiences, words and gestures of these non-professionals it weaves a kind of *théâtre verité*. This socially conscious approach could be seen as a reawakening of the polemical naturalism of Maxim Gorky, whose impact in the years leading up to the Russian Revolution is described here by Andrew Upton:

> It upset people; it made them think. It asked questions about power, society, justice, humanity – not only through its content, but through its form ... [Gorky] puts the powerless on stage and asks: if we are feeling this wrong about our world, why can't we do something about it?[1]

Weller does and asks exactly this with the Grassmarket Project's productions, each of which is trying to answer a question about the world we live in. It is this simple human act of asking people about their lives, Weller believes, that reveals social truths that no amount of imagination or speculation could invent. Each production starts with a question or a set of questions to uncover the truth about such issues as homelessness, youth offending, asylum seeking, mental illness or the sex trade.

So, audiences get to see and hear real homeless people in *Glad* speaking about their lives on the streets of Edinburgh, actual inmates from a Scottish young offenders institution

---

[1] Andrew Upton, 'Man of the People', *The Guardian*, 19 May 2007, http://www.guardian.co.uk/books/2007/may/19/theatre.stage (accessed 23 January 2013).

re-enacting their arguments and fights in *Bad*, former mental hospital patients reliving their breakdowns in *Mad* – the founding trilogy of startling dramas that then set a pattern of theatre-making here in the UK and, increasingly, abroad, in Europe, North America, Brazil and the Middle East.

Most if not all of these productions (re)present, in a mediated artistic form, extreme experiences of all kinds, revealing to a sometimes horrified audience just what it means to have tortured an enemy combatant (*Soldiers*) or to have been physically and mentally abused (*Mad*) or to have seen the bruised and beaten body of your twin brother found dead whilst in police custody (*20:52*). No solutions are offered at the end of these dramas and there is no closure to send the audience off in contented reflection.

In asking people who have actually been through these experiences to 'perform' them for an audience, Weller is drawing on another honourable tradition, perhaps best exemplified by the French film director Robert Bresson, who in a long career rarely used professional actors or worked from a polished script. Like Weller, he was aiming beyond artifice, as his book, *Notes on the Cinematographer* (1975), makes very clear: 'No actors. (No directing of actors.) No parts. (No learning of parts.) No staging. But the use of working models, taken from life. BEING (models) instead of SEEMING (actors).'[2]

Using a professional actor, Bresson felt, 'gives us an image of a human being that is too simple and thus false'. Authenticity is vital. Interestingly, he also privileged risk in the dramatic process – 'At each touch, I risk my life', he wrote in *Notes* – and chance and improvisation played a crucial role in shaping his films, as did limitations of budget. When asked why he imposed such difficulties on himself, he replied, 'In order to capture the real.' This, coupled with his dictum 'Make visible

---

[2] Robert Bresson, *Notes on the Cinematographer* (Copenhagen: Green Integer, 1997), p. 14.

what, without you, might perhaps never have been seen', all seems very pertinent indeed to Weller's whole project.

Plays like these throw down a gauntlet, not just to the people on stage to go beyond what they think they are capable of and not just to audiences expecting a comfortable night out at the theatre. They are also serious intellectual provocations. By blurring the divide between 'real life' and 'theatre', they question what counts as authentic performance. In bringing us face to face with the 'other', they interrogate our fonder notions of community in an attempt to heal our society's wounds. Ever since the initial production of *Glad*, the impact of this work has been recognised by participants, by audiences, by critics and by artists; the experience of seeing *Mad* gave budding playwright Sarah Kane the encouragement she needed to write *Blasted*, which defined the confrontational theatre of the 1990s: 'It changed my life because it changed me; the way I think, the way I behave. If theatre can change lives, then it can change society.'[3]

The relevance of Weller's project

The Grassmarket Project is not a traditional theatre company; it certainly does not fit into a West End model, as its productions are usually one-off, non-touring, short-run affairs. Up to quite recently, relatively few people in the mainstream theatre world have been aware of the company and its work and, when they do hear of its approach to working with non-professionals and the kind of subject matter it tackles, they often assume that it is a species of 'community theatre', a label that Weller is uncomfortable with. Although he rejects the idea of being called simply a 'maverick' – a subtle way, he believes, of sidelining the potential wider significance of

---

[3] Aleks Sierz, *In Yer Face Theatre: British Drama Today* (London: Faber and Faber, 2000), p. 93.

his work – he would also distance himself from mainstream community (or participatory) arts practice. This raises the question, of course, of what Weller and the Grassmarket Project are doing here.

In many ways, this enterprise is indeed a strange beast in a book about community-based and applied theatre. Some of the other companies considered here could be said broadly to subscribe to a common agenda and purpose, based on accepted ways of working. Few, if any, would take the kind of risks that Weller does with people (or communities) we normally only encounter below alarming headlines, such as young offenders, sex workers, would-be jihadists, immigrants, pregnant teenagers ... The Grassmarket Market is very much the Ancient Mariner at this wedding feast, with its wild, doomy tales making the guests a mite uncomfortable.

Like the mariner, Weller has been away from home for long periods: *The Foolish Young Man* was his first ever London-based production and the first (and so far only) show to secure funding from Arts Council England. Since the glory days of the Edinburgh Fringe, the company has, in fact, spent most of its time abroad. At the time of writing, Weller is developing a film project about street girls in Brazil and running theatre workshops in Afghanistan; the previous summer he worked with fifty teenagers from the Bronx at the invitation of the Knowledge is Power Programme.

With its plethora of foreign influences – Weller was once a student of Tadeusz Kantor, the avant-garde Polish director – and its recent excursions into film, with the support of another so-called maverick, Lars von Trier, what precise relevance does Weller's Grassmarket Project have for practitioners, teachers and students of theatre working now in this country? My answer would be: considerable. Weller's ongoing 'project' is, if nothing else, a great provocation to accepted ways of thinking about 'applied' or 'community theatre' – from the way he and his team engage with vulnerable non-professionals to the controversies the resulting productions generate amongst audiences to the questions all this raises about the purpose of theatre and performance itself.

This chapter explores these issues in two ways. First, largely through the lens of *The Foolish Young Man* (which I evaluated for the Calouste Gulbenkian Foundation in 2006), I examine the process involved in developing a Grassmarket production and the impact this had on its participants. My second consideration is the effect that the resulting public performance has on audiences and the connections that are forged between the community on stage and the wider world.

Their own truth

Understanding the process

In a society where success is measured by what we have, here is a guy who is rich and powerful, but he's kind of isolated, too, and bored with life. He is asking questions about how he feels about himself and his relationship to other people. To the young man he has seen panhandling on the street, for example – who is he? What does he feel? What is his life like? He wants to make contact with young people like these and they want to make contact with him, but it's a question of whether that relationship is possible. So the play turns on a question: What happens if we meet the 'others'?

Jeremy Weller

The Foolish Young Man ran for five sold-out performances at the Roundhouse Freedm Studios in Camden, north London, in June 2006. Around 600 people saw it live and many thousands more glimpsed scenes from it in Alan Yentob's profile of the company for the BBC documentary series *Imagine*. The play brought together a cast of ten local young people, aged fourteen to twenty-three, from multi-ethnic backgrounds, none of whom had ever acted on a professional stage before, together with David Harewood. Most of the young men were recruited from youth and drop-in centres while the women, who were younger, came from a local pupil referral unit. What they shared, according to Weller, was a disconnect from mainstream society: 'Their life is on the street and their contacts are in subcultural networks that are based on kinship, gang relationships, abuse, violence. They are drifting below the net, invisible.'

Each Grassmarket production has the same starting point: a question about contemporary society. Such questions proliferate in Weller's notebook, each the germ of a potential new play. Although answering the question might include desk research, the investigation is carried out largely through talking to people directly affected at the auditions or preliminary workshops run by the company to launch a new production.

While much participatory arts and theatre work, particularly with people considered vulnerable or 'at risk', avoids – on principle – any engagement with participants' personal histories, Weller instead encourages participants to talk about their lives in as much detail as they feel happy revealing. This often deeply personal, sometimes graphic material is the very stuff of which the drama – and the script – is to be constructed.

Talking about real life

At the 'audition' stage, no one is asked to perform pieces they have memorised or to read a script. What the company is looking for are not actorly qualities as such. Although presence and verbal confidence are important, it is, above all, 'emotional authenticity' that is desired. Jenle Hallund, Weller's long-term associate and company dramaturge, says that candidates 'have to have a certain vitality or rage or connection to life'.

In this production, the participants' energy and – sometimes – rage were palpable. The effort to create the necessary bond of trust with the young people and break down any prejudice they might have about theatre was a considerable challenge, as Weller admitted: 'It's like getting fourteen or fifteen mustangs corralled and ready to race in the right direction. But, if it works, it can be pretty magical.'

The first few weeks were a time for the company to listen to them and their stories and to begin building a working and informal relationship based on respect and empathy rather than a directive or more structured approach:

> The fact that you know that they are in this place right now but in a few weeks' time they are going to be somewhere different means that you are not going to start framing them and imprisoning them from day one. The level of anger – of feeling imprisoned in their own lives – is overwhelming. You have to really nurture them: find out who they are and play all the right tunes until they come to respect you or understand you or perhaps even like you. Then you *can* say yes and no to them, but you have got to be careful, because they are so used to abuse, so used to aggression, so used to people screaming at them.
>
> Jenle Hallund

As someone assisting with Grassmarket productions with young people over the years, Ian Mitchinson has observed how Weller encourages younger people to tell their stories:

> Jeremy's process is to treat these young people like human beings, listen to what they say and give them some validation. They think: *this is okay; these people are interested in us*. He's not looking at them like a project, asking them to answer questions or tick the appropriate boxes. They've shown up because they think it's worthwhile – they're getting positive feedback and they respond to that. They feel that what they've got to say is worth listening to.

The growth of community

One-to-one sessions support participants in retrieving and articulating personal experiences so that, when they are ready to, they can begin to try their stories out on others in the group. Gradually, as people begin to recognise what each has in common with the other, the confidence to tell their own story grows. That, in turn, inspires others to share more experiences. This happened, for example, right at the start of the second staging of *Mad*, according to one of the actors involved, Naomi Seekings: 'You're suddenly in this situation where someone's revealing a lot and you think: *ok, I'll reveal something as well.* The more trust there is, it just spirals.'

What emerges from this process is a sense of a community that often goes deeper than simply being members of the cast. The individual voice is still audible but it is set into a wider context, in which what might have remained documentary evidence – those solitary admissions and cries of pain – is transmuted into shared experience.

So, as the material produced by participants grows and deepens, it becomes more revelatory and thus more fully authentic. This is the material from which the script will grow and develop. Generated in a series of workshops and captured on video, the most dramatically promising material is transcribed and used as a guideline for developing dialogue during further workshop sessions. Participants are encouraged to develop and improvise their stories and their monologues on their own with Weller or Hallund or another company member, and then together, occasionally dramatising them in groups of two or three or four but mainly working on their own words. The creation of the script follows the improvised expression of the experience rather than, as is the case in conventional playwriting, emerging from the process of writing. The narrative is constructed partly through juxtaposition of different stories and speeches, the fragments that have been created in the auditions and later workshops. Visiting the workshop/rehearsals at various stages during the whole process, I saw how, at the same time as individual monologues and exchanges were honed and practised, Weller and Hallund laboured over where each part would fit, what linking scenes were needed to smooth over the joins, how the narrative would develop through moments of high drama and reflection to give some light and shade in such a bleak scenario.

> We might have four or five characters and we can see that this is what they are going to deliver in the show: this is the scene or the issue or the emotion that they are going to carry. When we have characters or experiences or situations that are solid, we encourage more improvisations to explore or contradict them. People worry about us just trying things out because they don't realise that it doesn't have to be good or make sense all the time. If it doesn't work, it doesn't work, so we try something else.

It seems to be a process of taking on board the logic of the young people's stories and seeing where they might lead in the larger tale, turning individual confessions into part of a bigger story with a bigger meaning. What then emerges is a psychological narrative rather than a plot driven by events. The action comes out of the catalytic effect of stories bumping into each other and creating sparks.

Improvisation continues right through the process as it can suggest more powerful ways of telling these stories. When final versions of monologues and dialogues emerged from the improvisations, they were translated into written text – a script. The young participants found their own words returned to them as lines to learn, although the company encouraged them to use the script more as an aide-mémoire than something to learn parrot-fashion.

There remained one further ingredient to add, in this case midway through the process. Even given the innate drama of many of the young people's stories, there might be a danger that, without a point of conflict, the material could simply end up as a documentary, convincing and even moving, perhaps, but inert and essentially undramatic. Enter David, the eponymous foolish young man.

Introducing the catalyst

A common device in Grassmarket productions is to bring into the community an interrogatory figure, often played by a professional actor, who represents a version of mainstream society (like the audience) and against whose conventional values the voices of the marginalised are set in contrast, protest or opposition. Setting one world into conflict with another acts as a catalyst and shapes the drama, which circles endlessly around the difficulty of communication. This outsider figure acts as a lightning rod. Naomi Seekings played one such interloper in *One Moment* (1993), a play set in an old people's home:

> I played this idealistic social worker who wanted to foment a revolution amongst the old people. I felt their unhappiness and I wanted to stoke the fire, as it were. I came across as a naïve, idealistic troublemaker. My intentions were good but they hadn't really been well thought out. I created the revolution but didn't quite know what to do with the mess that resulted.

David makes a similar misjudgement in *The Foolish Young Man*. He is equally naïve and rather less well meaning in his blindness to what these teenagers might need from people like him. This was illustrated by an anecdote told by Feras, one of the young performers and an ex-gang member, at a post-show discussion, when he was asked why he had pulled out a gun on David. 'It's because David's pushed him to that point. David ain't really done nothing, but at the end of the day he just makes me frustrated.'

Not being seen or listened to or recognised leads to frustration and, ultimately, fury.

As I said in one of my scenes to David: *You ain't ever been to my council estate and seen that same crackhead sitting on the same step with the same needle tapping on the same arm looking for the same vein.*

Interestingly, the slippage between the third and first person in Feras's first statement – referring to himself as both 'him' and 'me' – emphasises just how angry he feels *in real life* about the fact that the Davids of this world fail to respond to him. Equally, it also points to the impact on Feras and the other participants of the process they have been through – of, in effect, turning their own real life experiences into an 'act'. Weller explains what, he believes, changed Feras from a frightening 'street kid' into someone audiences could meet and chat to afterwards:

On stage, he could show his real vulnerability. He could share his inner self with an audience of strangers. People could get to know him, so he could get to know himself. He could drop his real 'role'. He could drop the street thug and the hooligan, and actually reveal himself: fragile, vulnerable, the same as you and me – seeking love, seeking tenderness. But if you'd said anything like that to him before, he'd have slashed you.

Commitment to the craft

Given the chaotic lives many of the young people led, with often little parental support and encouragement, it was remarkable how committed they were overall to the production, attending workshops and doing their best to be punctual and do what was required of them. By the final two weeks of rehearsals, the storyline was being performed twice each day – a demanding schedule for any actor, but considerably more so for these young non-professionals. One cast member, Safisha, looking back over the whole process, had this to say:

> For the last month and a half, my mind has been focused on this and nothing else. I haven't thought about sitting in my blocks with people that don't really do anything for me. I'm doing something that I'm enjoying and it's taken up most of my time. This half term I should be out doing what I normally do but I've been here rehearsing from, like, one o'clock till nine o'clock.

Safisha and the others had had a steep learning curve to climb, especially in turning their raw stories into performance, as David Harewood recognised:

> Because of their inexperience, they thought at the start that it was going to be easy – that all they would have to do is turn it up full volume, get angry and remember their lines. When you start to run through it a few times and you explain to them about the different colours and shades that they need, they start to think, *Actually this is more complicated than I thought it was going to be.* And then something else engages in their brain and they think, *I've actually got to work for this*, and it's like a dog with a bone: they don't want to let it go until they have it.

This learning breakthrough is well exemplified by what Luke achieved in the climactic scene with David, when he is told that he has to leave the flat. His reaction is vitriolic, moving swiftly from angry protest to a violent attack on David ending with the older man pinned down and Luke threatening a future settling of scores. David describes the way in which this scene finally came together:

> It's just so real that sometimes it's a bit scary. Does it feel safe? Totally, though at times it really doesn't look it. I mean Luke is a big guy ... At first I was just pushing him to get angry with me but he just wouldn't do it and I knew why – because he was scared of losing his temper. It took about three weeks of me telling him not to worry and that I

trusted him. I was physically pushing him, just trying to get him to hit the red line, but he wouldn't do it. And then, one day, he did the scene – he frightened the fuck out of me! He grabbed me, pushed me up against the wall and he was scary, but it was safe. As soon as we finished, I said, *Well done, that was great.* He went, *Oh, right* – that's *how you do it,* because he knew then he could trust himself.

By the time of the performances, David was full of praise for all the young performers:

Today, I just knew that they were starting to understand the process of playing. They now have the confidence to improvise live in front of an audience. Professional actors would find that difficult. I don't know whether it's because they are fresh to it but it's just so *honest* working with these guys. They haven't got the sophistication of people in the business, in terms of voice and diction and all the technicalities that make up a professional actor, but – because they have none of that – they are uninhibited.

Self-knowledge through performance

Although shaping text and utterance, using gesture and the body and many other aspects of acting are part of what engages participants, the learning goes much deeper than this. The big claim that Weller makes for the company's methodology is that, by acting out on stage the role they play in real life, participants can be transformed. By turning their persona into a character, their stories into a script to be learned and rehearsed, their experiences into an entertainment for a theatre audience, participants achieve a new perspective by, in effect, looking at themselves in the third person.

By encouraging people to present a public performance of their own experiences, however disguised or edited, the company hopes to create the opportunity for them to step back from their daily lives and see themselves, as it were, from a distance – as others might see them. Not only does this process give participants the opportunity to reflect on their lives and how their experiences have shaped (or distorted) them, but it also – in theory – enables them to step out of role in their real lives just as they do when they come off stage and take greater control of their lives.

Having witnessed a long rehearsal, Simon Richey, then Director of Education at the Calouste Gulbenkian Foundation, observed how it had benefited the young people

> to distance themselves from their characters, to slip between their real selves and their characters, as it were, a small piece of fiction so that they might observe and begin to understand the feelings and impulses of those 'characters' that were almost, but not quite themselves.

One of the concerns that some have about this work, however, is that, in making art out of trauma, the company is somehow exploiting its participants and, worse still, in not constructing alternative scenarios but re-enacting the tragic truths of their existence on a public stage, fails to offer them any hope of escape or redemption.

Facing down the risks

There is no gainsaying that the whole process is fraught with risk, evident right from the start and still tangible in the final performance, where it often feels to the audience as if anything could kick off. Participants undoubtedly risk a lot by revealing hidden truths about themselves to others, first to the artists, then to their peers in the cast and ultimately to an audience of total strangers. It does not always work and not all the young people selected to participate stayed the course. One young woman, chosen for her courage in relating at her audition how she had been raped as a young child, was given a lot of support but, unable to manage her violent behaviour, ultimately ended up – tragically – in a young offenders' institution. The company has to be aware of the line between giving people a chance to explore their experiences and where more formal, professional help will be needed; there are limits, according to Hallund:

> They only give us what they want to give us and, if we then feel that it is too much or too dark, we will stop them, because there are certain things that are too volatile or too emotional to deal with here.

Sociologist Halla Beloff believes, as do other supporters of Weller's approach, that those who take part in his productions are, *ipso facto*, survivors:

> Nobody goes to work for Jeremy who doesn't want to; nobody tells stories in public that they don't want to. At any stage of the game during those long rehearsal periods, everyone knows exactly what's going to be happening.

As someone with a positive experience of the process, Naomi Seekings explains how it can help people to confront and deal with a painful experience:

> It comes to a point where you've spoken about it, you've re-enacted it, you've got someone else to play you, you've recreated the situation, you've fantasised maybe about what you would have said in that scenario, you've really dissected it and played with it and so it is removed from you and it becomes *material*.

This seemed to be the case for the young cast members I spoke to. Sharing their difficult experiences and feelings here did not seem to exacerbate their pain but, if anything, tended to alleviate it, as Luke reflects:

We're spending a lot of time together, improvising lots of different scenes. Some of it is about my life, some isn't, some is embellished. Most of the play is taken from our personal experiences and we've just mashed them altogether. These are experiences that have changed us or meant a lot to us. When you're in this environment, it makes it easier to express those things, maybe. I've never really had anyone to talk to about any of this stuff, so perhaps it helps to deal with some of the shit people have to go through.

For Feras, although less familiar than his estate, from which he rarely dared to stray, the space provided by the company was somewhere he could feel less at risk:

In here you know you're safe. You know nothing ain't going to happen to you and you can act it out and be or do whatever you want. But out there, when you're having that experience, you don't know what's going to happen.

Weller believes that his approach facilitates the difficult process that people actually have to go through 'to reach that point where everything is good'. For him, too many participatory projects leave people 'spinning on a wheel', making little lasting impact on their everyday lives. For the young people in *The Foolish Young Man*, the 'only way to escape their antisocial roles is to explore them and talk about them and, ultimately, explode them':

We are so afraid of tackling these issues head on and saying: *Well, who* are *you? Tell me about it, show me your rage, show me your hurt.* Without going through all this shit, how on earth can they escape their roles? And if we don't listen to them, how can we understand what they are going through? I think we are really afraid of listening to the reality of these kids. And they are afraid of dealing with their own emotions because those are seen as taboo.

While Weller and his company listen to the reality, the participants themselves have to do the heavy lifting. It is not a question of the Grassmarket Project doing something 'for' these people on the margins but enabling them to experience and discover for themselves who they are and who they might be. This was the point right from the first production:

> Why did I do *Glad*? It was not to cure the men of their various addictions and dependencies. But rather I intended to find the truth of their experience – not my truth of their experience but rather their own truth. This is more complex, because it relies on them reflecting upon the role that they play to others and the role that they play for themselves. This was very important to me and it was a major part of my investigation.

*

Jeremy is doing something similar to a director like Robert Lepage – showing art being created before your eyes. He sidesteps the risk of turning it all into a visit to the zoo, where people gawp at the dispossessed, by making it an act of ownership: the plays are absolutely owned by the people making them – and discovering themselves in the process. It's not about doing social work – though art often is extremely good social work, often the best. Art *can* save people.

Lyn Gardner

A wounding process

The impact on the audience

The first night of *The Foolish Young Man* was one of the most immediate and edgy theatre performances I have ever seen. The group of talented young actors brought together by Grassmarket created a sense of raw realism so convincing that you had to remind yourself at times that this was a rehearsed performance. It felt more like eavesdropping on the real lives of young people living at or near the margins and struggling to cope with some really difficult issues. The emotional response the performance evoked in the audience was real and spontaneous. People came out stunned, realising they had witnessed something remarkable.

Ben Emmerson QC

Weller's is a theatre where the voice is authentic because the lines the voice is speaking have been lived in, in a way beyond the reach of the most dedicated exponent of the Method. This was evident even during rehearsals, when a youth worker was so shocked by the screaming row between Kasha and another actor that she ran forward to hug her and calm her down, whereupon the whole cast broke into laughter. Kasha explained: *We're just acting.*

It is this authenticity that gives his productions their peculiar power to convince – and often unsettle – a theatre audience. Weller believes that presenting 'the density of life' denies spectators the comfort of 'mimesis' – a recognisable version of what they already know.

Because these authentic voices come from the dispossessed and marginalised, they bring a whiff of danger into what has become, essentially, a middle-class space – and sometimes more than a whiff. Anything could happen if you bring young offenders or homeless people onto the stage and permit them to speak their minds, to be themselves. There is a fear that what is happening on stage could actually get out of hand or even spill over into the audience. Weller cites Luke's assault on David as an example of this:

The convention in theatre is that: here's the stage and there's the audience. If you take that away and have your players somehow in the same domain as the people watching them, that makes it very scary. If Luke comes out and he's right next to the audience and he goes *you fucking idiot* to David – and David's us after all – and then he grabs him and says *I'll fucking cut you*, you know he really has done that kind of thing. And then he slams him against the wall and you can hear the audience moan. So, you're breaking emotional borderlines and taking them out of the safety zone into a realm of physical danger.

The impact on an audience's feelings can be considerable. Witnessing *Mad*, Sarah Kane wrote:

It was an unusual piece of theatre because it was totally experiential as opposed to speculatory. As an audience member, I was taken to a place of extreme mental discomfort and distress and then popped out the other end. What I did not do was sit in the theatre considering as an intellectual conceit what it might be like to be mentally ill.[4]

What theatre critic Lyn Gardner terms the audience's *discovery* of people's lives in Grassmarket productions is of a different order to what might be called its *recognition* of similar characters represented by professional actors. For example, an audience watching a Royal Court play about young gang members will come away 'thinking to themselves that they've learned something about those lives – that they have become, in a sense, "experts" on the subject'. That comfortable intellectual distancing is not possible with a Grassmarket production. Indeed, for some audience members, watching a play like *Mad* feels like being personally attacked. Although the usual line that divides the audience from the action on stage remains intact – there is no attempt at audience participation – the interaction between the two has become so

---

[4]Quotation from Graham Saunders, '"Just a Word on a Page and there is the Drama": Sarah Kane's theatrical legacy', *Series litteraires* (10 March 2003), excerpted in Sierz, *In Yer Face Theatre*, p. 92.

highly charged that audience members feel directly challenged
and engaged – or repelled. Beloff describes the impact of her
own experience of *Mad*:

> The women were so histrionic, in every sense of the word.
> They had these amazing stories about abuse and drugs and
> drink and they were screaming and shouting. My sister
> just shrivelled up – not only had she never seen anything
> like that, she'd never heard anything like that and she just
> couldn't bear it. Jolly good, we thought, she should learn.
> Intellectually, I knew these things went on and we gave
> money to Women's Aid and so on, but to actually *see* these
> stories enacted in front of you was really shattering.

The question of voyeurism

The main charge made against these plays is that of voyeurism:
making a spectacle out of these victims of society for our entertainment. Weller is frank that there is 'a definite voyeurism
involved' but that it is inevitable in a fragmented society like
ours, where 'we have removed ourselves, step by step, from
the "other"':

> If you build that wall and then you open a door in it to
> show what lies behind, *of course* voyeurism is involved.
> But if it takes you up close and personal to a reality you
> know nothing about, that's actually a chance to learn
> and be enriched, not to be turned on or to feel yourself
> even more removed. And, actually, the audience's usual
> response has always reassured me that it's not voyeuristic
> in the perverted sense, because in the end they feel more
> knowledge and more empathy for the 'other'. They've seen
> how the 'other' lives, they've seen how the 'other' feels.

Audience members are opened up in a way that disturbs
them. Even those who feel positive about what they have seen

are, in Naomi's words, 'fuelled, charged with emotion and thoughts of how wrong things are in the world, full of surges of emotion and feelings about how you might change things'. For Bellof, this is not catharsis but 'something you should take away with you and keep: it's not a healing but a *wounding* process'.

Jenle Hallund argues that *feeling* is important if one is concerned with social justice. Intellectual understanding and rational argument will only take you so far. Emotional understanding is made possible by showing the audience over the hour and a half they are sat there how the same issues – hurt, love, neglect, fear – are 'not conditions for one part of our society but conditions for all of us, including these people on stage with whom you thought you had no connection'. The audience's view of the world and how to categorise the people in it has been exploded. The 'others' have been made visible.

Just as Weller encourages his actors to dig deep to discover the truth about themselves and to comprehend the reasons for the extreme situation they find themselves in, so he provides the audience with a unique opportunity to examine its own social conscience:

> I want to reveal the other as not distant or separate from us, but actually one and the same. I want people to feel closer to them. And, therefore, to be closer to those aspects of themselves that they might otherwise deny, which might either be their dark side – actually feeling that they have to remove themselves further – or their innate desire to help, to be a good Samaritan.

David, the foolish young man, who is the point of identification for the middle-class theatregoers in the audience, starkly represents the darker side. The shifts in his attitudes – and his ultimate failure – implicate the wider society that has failed these young people.

Putting the audience on the spot

David's self-made success, embodied in the inanimate form of his smart apartment, can be seen as a triumph of his 'running' from the past which, as a black man, could encompass the history of enslavement as well as his own personal background. What he seems dimly aware of at the start of the play is that he has also *forgotten* that past in some way. The potential for a fall into social failure, presumably even greater for someone already marginalised by white power structures and ever struggling for recognition, is now made flesh by the waifs and strays he takes in.

David's initial motivations seem mixed. Partly, he has a simple, if misguided, hope that these new relationships will be stimulating. Having surrounded himself with the trappings of material success, he is dimly aware that something is missing in his life, which we might call human intimacy. As a paid-up member of a society that stereotypes and exoticises its 'others', he is also titillated by taking such a risk, as if he were conducting a social experiment of some kind with these young strangers.

As David discovers more and more disquieting information about these young people's lives, he senses another role he might begin to play, as a benefactor. Although by no stretch of the imagination a typical 'do-gooder', David does share some of the do-gooder's unearned sense of confidence that they can handle the problem. He believes that he can offer these young people something of an example, as a self-made black man with material wealth and a good social position. His mistake is to assume that material things are all that is needed to satisfy these young people's needs.

He is, however, quickly disabused of any such charitable instincts, ultimately recoiling from the social truths he is exposed to as well as from the immediate dangers these young people represent, with their sudden bouts of violence and their drug abuse. And, at the point when his mastery of the situation is finally demonstrated to be illusory, he steps back from the brink and refuses to save them. He has recognised what these young people represent to him personally: a 'remembering' he would rather forget.

This is most evident when Jahmal gives a heartrending account of his racial and sexual abuse as a young man of colour; this moves David to tears. At this critical point, empathy and recognition seem possible but David ultimately refuses them, declaring: 'I am not your father.' By running and not bearing responsibility, he becomes, as Luke warns him at the end, a 'marked man' – as Cain was marked by God and cast out as a fratricide. David's is a tragic fall: hubris rewarded with the promise of a violent death. Weller sums it up:

> The world that the kids brought to him was all about emotion and pain and the things that have been done to them. And they said to him: *I was abused, my mother didn't love me, I've got nowhere, I'm homeless, I'm an illegal immigrant. Help me.* And what did he say? He went – *Well, here's ten quid. I'm not your dad. Get out!* Quite often that's how society responds.

Weller's work, therefore, not only shows the audience people they have not properly seen before, which is quite a shock in itself, but by placing, as it were, a member of the audience on stage as an external observer and catalyst of the drama, it implicates them in a situation of social (dis)order that they feel, to some degree or other, complicit in.

This effect is deepened by the fact that the suffering ones are those who are speaking a version of their own real histories and experiences, while the outsider is the only fully fictional figure, standing in for the hungry imagination of the audience. Those who are generally stereotyped and labelled as criminal or insane or corrupt hold all the information we, as the audience, need to know. Thus, whatever roles the young people in *The Foolish Young Man* have created for themselves in order to survive, they are not those prescribed for them by mainstream society. In their own terms, they are authentic creatures and thus a vivid contrast to the self-deluded observers from the comfortable classes. The power relationship has shifted, at least in this space and for this duration, and the effect on the audience is almost always electrifying and often disturbing.

The bigger picture

Weller seeks out people for his productions who have that rawness of emotion we often associate with people who are struggling with life – people who, as Jenle Hallund puts it, 'will not be manipulated or socially corrected into a workable or a "successful" role' in society – as part of his bigger project: a moral critique of our dominant values. People who are suffering in life are, in some way, carrying – and revealing – the condition of our times. This is the reason that Jeremy Weller is drawn to 'socially excluded' people: because they embody that conflict. They are not comfortable abstractions.

By putting these hitherto invisible people on stage, Weller smashes the 'mirrors of distorting glass' so that we, the audience, can see who these people really are, in all their complex humanity. The young people we see and get to know in *The Foolish Young Man* are no longer mere 'figments' of a tabloid imagination but suffering flesh and blood. The tales of muggings and sudden violence on the streets begin to seem less arbitrary when we see and hear their stories.

What is enacted on stage is a radical topsy-turvydom, where the outcast becomes the centre of authority and truth. David's fall at the end of *The Foolish Young Man* reveals the true social outcast to be, not the young gang member or the juvenile delinquent, but the respectable man who, in the end, refuses to recognise their shared history and predicament – their common humanity.

7

Rosemary Lee

Interview and introduction by Martin Welton

Rosemary Lee is one of the UK's leading independent chore-ographers. Since the late 1980s she has created dance works across a range of scales and genres, including film (*boy*, 1995; *Infanta*, 1998), gallery installations (*Remote Dancing*, 2004), site-specific and large-scale participatory works (*New Springs from Old Winters*, 1987; *Haughmond Dances*, 1990; *Ascending Fields*, 1992; *Banquet Dances*, 1999) as well as theatrical presentations (*Charged*, 1997; *Passage*, 2001). She is an associate artist of ResCen at the University of Middlesex, a Work Place artist and, currently, is the South East Dance Fellow.

Much of the inspiration for her work is found in the stuff of human relations. In choreographies that are often as profound as they are breathtakingly simple in their execution and design, she has repeatedly asked after the means by which, despite differences of age, gender or background, audiences and performers might find a sense of togetherness, or belonging in a common ground. Although she has often worked with mixed casts of professional and non-professional performers, or featuring intergenerational companies, Lee has largely resisted efforts to place her work under the aegis of community or participatory performance.

An example of this is given by *Common Dance*, a work made by Lee as a commission for the Dance Umbrella festival and Greenwich Dance Agency at Greenwich Borough Hall in south-east London. The resultant performance, had a company of fifty three mostly non-professional performers aged between eight and eighty-three. They were accompanied by a choir of young people from the Finchley Young People's Music Group and a bagpiper, performing music composed by Terry Mann. Exploring the social and environmental themes of a 'common ground', *Common Dance* was described by *The Observer*'s dance critic Sanjoy Roy as 'revelatory – like seeing both a wood and its trees'.

FIGURE 12 *Rosemary Lee,* Common Dance *(2009). Photo: Simon Weir.*

The interview that follows is part of an ongoing conversation since the staging of *Common Dance* between Lee and Martin Welton, a theatre studies academic, which led to a one-day symposium, *On Taking Care*, at Queen Mary, University of London in December 2012. Co-curated by Welton and Lee, the symposium saw the launch of an interactive DVD reflecting on the creative process of making *Common Dance*, but also involved contributions from medical and social work professionals, environmentalists and artists in an effort to develop a wider debate about care in society, the environment and art. At the time of writing, this conversation and debate is continuing, not least in Lee's own choreography. As she suggests in the interview that follows, hers is an approach to performance that entreats audiences and dancers alike, to pay attention to one another, with care.

MW: Common Dance was the first large-scale work with a company of performers not directly involved in professional dance that you had made for some time. How does it relate to earlier pieces that you've made on a similar scale or with similar groups of performers?*

RL: There's a strong relationship between *Common Dance* and older work with casts of over fifty performers. The first one I made was in 1987, *New Springs from Old Winters*, in Oxford Town Hall. It was a civic building so had a similar feel and although there wasn't a stage, you could have an audience with a similar kind of relationship to the cast as you could in Greenwich Dance. When I made *Common Dance* in 2009, I felt ready to revisit some of the older work, and quite consciously revisited and drew things out from those works and distilled them again.

I think that as a young choreographer I was encouraged that every piece you made had to be new and different, which was ridiculous in a way, because we know that artists have a signature in a sense: they can try to go away from that, but there's going to be something authorial about it. I think I felt,

'Right, I'm not going to worry that this is wrong to do now I'm in my fifties, I'm going to make a work that goes back in time and draws things out of some of the works that I made in the past that I feel are worth revisiting.'

The piece I made just before *Common Dance* that was on an equal scale was for about seventy-five people in the Painted Hall in Greenwich and it was also orchestrated by Greenwich Dance. *Banquet Dances* was part of a trilogy of pieces called *Take Me to the River*. The audience went up the Thames in a boat and they would drop off at Greenwich, then Canary Wharf and then the South Bank. It was a really lovely idea. I always wanted to go back to Greenwich Dance to work with them; I loved the way they supported the project, I loved their ethos.

One of the striking things about Common Dance *is not just the number of people that you encounter on the stage and that they're clearly different genders, of different ethnic backgrounds, but also their age range. Was that a choice – 'I think I'd like to make a piece across a scale of ages' – or was it something that developed more thematically as you began to think through what to make?*

I think a bit of both really. All the other works have had a similar age range, even some pieces that don't have big casts: in *Remote Dancing*, a video installation, the ages go from eight to seventy-four. Thematically, I'm interested in trying to make work that spans the generations because I'm fascinated by our life cycle. I'm fascinated by people who are nearer their birth and by people who are nearer their death even though not everybody follows a pattern of living to a certain age. I am interested in life and death.

In Common Dance, *at least*, *there are cyclical themes: I was wondering if the age range and the social mix of people in it allowed the audience to find itself reflected somehow and that that is why the piece picked up the community/participatory*

performance label so easily. That's quite an unusual sense of
engagement with theatre dance, perhaps because there's very
often a kind of virtuosic element to it. You watch it and you're
watching that virtuosity, or you're watching the performance
of technique. That's not to say that either of those things were
absent from Common Dance *but you also had a sense of*
connection to the collective on stage.

The connection with the audience is different if you are
watching young, virtuosic dancers. There's something different
there, it's not about you and your participation or your
experience in your body so much. I've always wanted to make
work that connected with a wider range in the audience and
with people that weren't in the know, without that meaning
that I have to dumb down the work in any way. I want to
make work that a lot of different people could get something
out of, but that doesn't mean I have to make it easier in any
way. I struggle with elitist work. Even though I will go to
theatre and pay a big price for a ticket, because I want to
see the work, I don't want to be in that place myself. That's
something to do with not wanting to be some sort of luxury.
I see the arts as necessities and if I believe that, then I feel I've
got to make work that is necessary somehow as well – does
that make sense?

Absolutely. Maybe that sense of willingness to chuck form to
one side, or to step beyond the perceived restrictions of form
and to be socially informed in doing so, is somehow reflective
of your training, maybe through the work of Laban?

When I was at the Laban Centre I didn't study the work
of Laban himself that deeply, but you could feel it in the
building: it infused some of the work. We were being trained
to be dancers rather than Laban practitioners *per se*. What it
did teach me was the whole notion of art for everybody, that
everybody can have some kind of input into a creative practice
and that everybody's creative. I came with an interest in that

sort of thing, but the Laban Centre also helped me develop it. I was taught by Peter Brinson, who's quite a name in the dance world. He was a balletomane really, but he was a thoughtful balletomane and he taught us sociology and we read a bit of Marx and we read Heidegger and Descartes. We were looking at the role of the arts in society, through dance. He was responsible for projects like *Ballet for All* which involved ballet dancers going out into schools.

In terms of my background with respect to community performance, I've also been very influenced by things like amateur dramatics and pantomime that I did in my childhood. I learnt a lot about participatory projects through amateur dramatics, and I learnt a lot about how to be inclusive in my ballet school, how you make sure everybody's involved and you don't have stars and you don't favouritise. I grew up with a strong sense of what that felt like. I also come from a Quaker background on one side and I spent my gap year at an international studies centre in Birmingham, living in a community of Quakers who were welcoming revolutionaries and people going back to their countries to try to initiate pacifist change and peaceful revolution. So I grew up believing that you're on this earth to do something good, and I really think that is absolutely in my DNA.

Would you want to embrace or resist a suggestion that Common Dance *was a community or a participatory project?*

I think I resist labels just because I'm not very good at being part of a club and there's a bit of me that is resistant to being boxed in by something. Also, if I become a community artist, whatever that might mean, I worry that that sort of ring-fences me into a way of working that doesn't then allow me to hop to another place. I want to be seen as working in lots of different ways. I have the same overall aim, but I love to make work for the stage or (for the sake of a better word) high art settings, such as galleries, equally to making work that involves fifty people. I suppose that what I would say is that when my work involves larger casts, or casts of people without professional training, what I'm doing is trying to illustrate community, or to reveal what community might mean or could be. But I wouldn't say that I'm a typical community arts practitioner, especially in the theatre world. I don't really devise the work with the group. I create it with them. It's slightly different.

There's also the question of different sorts of audience that comes with that way of working. When you were making Common Dance, who was the audience in your head?

A really good question. I knew I was going to get a lot of people in – people's relatives and others who know them, and there was a choir as well – but I worry about that because a lot of people might think that's why you do this kind of project. I really don't work like that at all. I'm thinking that 'yes, so-and-so's granny might be there', but that'll be great because that's an older person who might not necessarily see work like this. That's more how I'd see it, rather than 'I've got a ready-made audience.' I also really want to attract the kind of audience who might see it as a work of art, looking at it in the same way as they might look at something in a more stereotypical theatre, let's say. If it's labelled as community art then there's some baggage that goes with that, which I think is really unfortunate.

I mean, in Britain we're known for our community dance and how brilliant it is. I'm very much part of that as an advocate, and I'm quite involved with Foundation for Community Dance as well, and I have been all through my career. When I was a younger choreographer I was making work for youth theatres, going round the country doing *ad hoc* performances that gathered casts in different towns. I think it's fantastic that there's this kind of work in this country that's involving people and enriching their lives. But equally, because we have that kind of movement I think there can be a problem about who fits where, and who is what, and that's why I want to first and foremost see myself as a maker, an artist: rather than saying this is the way I make work and that it follows a methodology that's the same as someone else's.

I think that I also have a very strong sense of justice and fairness so I struggle through life, wanting to sort of make things fair – because life isn't. Through things like *Common Dance* and hopefully the other works I've made, I am really striving to make it apparent that people are equal. So therefore the whole structure of what I'm making, everything about it, how they come into the room, how there's cups of tea for them, how they're credited in the programme, how they're costumed, how they dance through the piece, and their individual journeys through the piece are all equal in importance. Everyone is vitally important to the piece: that's fundamental to the way I like to work.

I want to ask you about the process of making Common Dance. *You had quite a lot of thematic and textual material assembled beforehand, and then only a limited amount of time with the cast, right? So what did you prepare in advance, and how did that then feed into the work that you made over that summer?*

The way I worked on *Common Dance* became a bit of a model for how I've worked on the next large-scale piece, *Square Dances* [2011]. I had at least a year of sort of pottering and ruminating about the whole theme of *Common Dance*. I knew I wanted to make a work that was about commonality or what we have in common, but also to keep that word very loose, thinking about connection, community, communication, communion and common land – which is quite an English term. All of those strands were coming into the work and *New Springs from Old Winters* also had a similar feeling of drawing people to a big space to be together, although it was really looking at rituals of darkness, of light, of winter going into spring and so on.

How were the dancers recruited?

I'd done a lot of research and thinking and had a lot of images together in my head. When I assembled the cast I knew I could fit about fifty people on that stage comfortably all at once, and I knew I needed a range that was really even in age and gender. I think this is true for almost all my work, but I was also looking for people who were able to really taste the movement and have an openness in the way they experienced it. They had to be able to really live it and be energised by a tasting of its quality – they needed to be able to work quite qualitatively. It wasn't important to me whether they could learn a routine, because I don't ever do that, but it was important that they could make an image live in themselves and have it make sense to them, have it speak to them. So I made sure that I got all that in advance, through some initial workshops. Then I had a weekend where I tried out lots of different ideas. Then I planned it as best I could with what I call the 'black holes', but with a sense of what the beginning might be, how it might open, how it might end, what kind of qualities would be in the first section, what kind of qualities in the middle, and so on. The company would meet me one evening and most weekends for about seven weeks: there was very little time because they're mostly working people. I had to plan, I couldn't possibly do any sort of devising. I had to know that that group's coming in that door when this word is sung and they're going to cross and they're going to do something while they cross. So I had things mapped out that I'd then try. There was a bit of devising going on in the evenings, but at the weekends it was more like, 'let's try this', 'this is what we're going to do', 'this piece has to do this here', and so on. So even if it was just 'I want some sort of rushing thing here', I would know that that's what I was going to have and mostly I didn't divert from that. So yes, a lot was planned and I had a team of four professionals and four apprentices. I had a few days with them before the whole process began to try things out and to explain how I teach, and how I wanted them to be with people.

A lot of the method is all about practicality – you've got fifty people, and you split them into four groups. That's four units of around thirteen people per unit. You can easily transmit ideas to thirteen people, they can work together, and I can choreograph thinking 'Where's that group gone? Oh, it's coming through that door.' I knew what I needed to do to make it actually viable. Also, the music, the lyrics and the libretto were all collated and assembled the year before as Terry Mann, the composer needed to make it ready for the choir to rehearse. We didn't get a huge amount of time to rehearse with them, but it was enough in the end because the choir is so strong. Even though I'd known them for years, standing in the middle of them, singing with them, it was so powerful and so beautiful. I just thought, oh God, now I get it! We all stepped up a bit at that point I think, and it helped a lot of the dancers free their voice.

I'd like to ask you about the afterlife of the piece. Since Common Dance *was performed you've made an interactive DVD that describes the process of producing it, and launched it with a one-day symposium in December 2012, which had a really extraordinary range of contributors. I wonder firstly why both the symposium and the DVD came to have the title* On Taking Care; *how did that theme of care come about in relation to* Common Dance *and also in a much wider discussion including nurses, doctors and academics?*

It's going to be quite a big answer, but ...

It was a very big question!

I think that I'm drawn to working with dancers, and in dance, because things can be left unsaid that are difficult you can investigate how you can connect better. If you can connect well, I think that you can care well. And so I feel that caring for someone is about connecting, is about empathising – for want of a better word – but also about understanding them on some level, and that understanding does not need to be of specific belief systems, it's something else. I think that dance is an art form that somehow speaks to your aliveness, it makes you feel more alive. I'm sure that's true of all art forms, but I think you could argue that dance, because it involves your body, somehow reminds you of your existence and your being alive. In order to dance well and in order to rehearse well, dancers need to have a balance of acceptance of leading and following, of letting go of control, of being in control, or of being just a partner. Just to pick someone up, just to dance with someone you've got to kind of understand how they're feeling at that moment. There's an ability to connect with people non-verbally and to be empathetic that's really attuned in a dancer, especially in the kind of dance world I'm interested in.

What's seemed clear to me looking across all the stages of the work is that the relationship between dance and care is not metaphorical, it's grounded, and embodied, but also manages to connect beyond its individual moment. So on the one hand there was the DVD record, but for the symposium you also commissioned some other artworks, if not in response to the piece, then certainly to the ideas that grew out of it. How did you go about curating that?

I wanted to involve artwork that isn't specifically made because it's been a community commission or isn't even necessarily made in a context like a hospital. There's loads of that work going on which I think is brilliant, but I wanted to draw attention to some artists' work that has, I would say, a more philosophical notion of care. It's often about the care of the audience member and their experience, in a kind of conceptual way. In them there's some sort of profound sense of thinking about what that care is for them, or what it might be like caring for, or honouring a stranger. If I describe Graeme Miller's work in *Beheld*, that's an installation that I would say is honouring, or at least reminding us, of the presence of an unknown stowaway who died falling from a plane. It's almost like the Tomb of the Unknown Warrior, which I also love: might we, as a society, take care of someone when we have no idea who they are, their background or what brought them here? This kind of work also has a respectful way of encouraging an audience to connect to that unknown, unnamed person. I think that there is an extraordinary attentiveness there that I find beautiful. I also think that this whole question of attentiveness is what we felt was at the root of what good care is, or what care might be, and the work I make is always about drawing attention to something, or about being attentive.

I think that's right, but I think that it's also quite a rare, unusual thing in some ways, and it was one of the things that was so powerful about Common Dance *ultimately, and why the woman behind me was weeping so profoundly at the end of it. As a society we're very rarely open, and really paying attention to one another, even in our day-to-day relationships. To find that in such a public way in* Common Dance, *the generosity of it, the revelation, and the sense that it was opening you up at the same time was profoundly moving.*

FIGURE 13 *Rosemary Lee,* Common Dance *(2009). Photo: Simon Weir.*

Thank you, I think it's something that I have to be a little bit careful of, but what I'm trying to do is to help people to open doors and to feel less constricted by having to fit in. It's not just my role in making the dance that does it, it's your seeing children and older people there together, doing the same thing, and the fact that they must have worked together. You're also seeing yourself, because there are middle-aged women, there are older women, there are older men, you're seeing yourself in your life. You're placing yourself with those people where you are in your life. We've still got to go out into the world afterwards, but hopefully that attention that the performers give each other has touched us, and we can see that there's potential for moments or elements of it to help us live our lives and believe in something.

8

The witness and the replay: London Bubble

Louise Owen

In 2012, London Bubble Theatre Company celebrated its fortieth anniversary. Like Hull Truck and Red Ladder, both founded in 1968, and the Natural Theatre Company, founded in 1970, London Bubble is one of the few companies emerging in the culture of 'alternative theatre' of that period that is still in operation. In the 1970s and 1980s, the Bubble Theatre, as it was then known, visited public parks across London, seeking to offer 'the excitement and anticipation of a 1970s type "circus" coming to town and hav[ing] something in its repertoire to appeal to everyone'.[1] According to Glen Walford, its first artistic director, the Bubble's portable 'tent' then represented 'the UK's only completely mobile theatre structure'.[2] The Bubble performed theatrical adaptations of film and fiction,

---

[1] *Greater London Arts Magazine*, October 1971. Quoted in Tony Rowlands, *Castles in the Park: the Bubble Theatre Company 1972–84* (unpublished dissertation, University College Swansea, 1985), p. 2.

[2] Glen Walford | Biography, http://www.glenwalford.com/pages/biog.html (accessed September 2012).

new plays, and productions of works by Beckett, Shakespeare and Brecht in tens of London boroughs during the course of a summer season, making week-long appearances in public space that today might be framed as 'pop-up theatre'. Its current 'mission', meanwhile, is to 'provide the artistic direction, skills, environment and resources to create inspirational, inclusive, involving theatre, which shares stories that animate the spaces of the city and the spirits of its citizens',[3] values which informed the company's outdoor promenade, site-specific, education and participatory work during the 2000s, when I worked there. In a twenty-first-century context in which 'community' and 'participation' are routinely coupled, this work is more readily recognisable as 'community theatre'.

But, at all points in its history, the company's main target constituency has been people who do not ordinarily go to the theatre, or make performance themselves. Its founding agenda of accessing 'new audiences' far from the cultural concentrations of the West End and its later focus on partici-patory projects each position the Bubble within a domain of community practice. Like the Bubble's own identity, the contours of this domain have been, and continue to be, far from stable. The multiplicity of art-forms, methodologies and political positions falling under the rubric of 'community', all in dialogue with cultural policy changes, have entailed the field's uneven metamorphosis and expansion in Britain since the 1960s. Written histories reflect this metamorphosis. Andrew Davies' *Other Theatres* (1987), for example, did in fact designate the Bubble's work 'community theatre' – meaning, simply, 'relationships with audiences'[4] – writing that its 'Shakespearean adaptations in London parks [possessed] an irreverence smacking of the penny gaffs'.[5] Yet the Bubble's

[3]London Bubble | Mission, http://www.londonbubble.org.uk/page/mission/ (accessed September 2012).
[4]Andrew Davies, *Other Theatres: The Development of Alternative and Experimental Theatre in Britain* (London: Macmillan Education, 1987), p. 175.
[5]Ibid., p. 185.

format resonated, too, with the efforts Davies attributed to 'political theatre' companies like Joint Stock and 7:84, of 'tak[ing] drama back to the people, touring and playing in front of audiences who had never been theatregoers'[6] – companies whose campaigning political programme the Bubble did not share. In *Dreams and Deconstructions: Alternative Theatre in Britain* (1980), Sandy Craig likewise drew attention to these affinities, but defined community theatre as a vehicle of 'community expression'[7] which addressed '"popularity" in the context of a particular locality and by seeking to become central, as opposed to peripheral, in the network of relations in that locality'.[8]

Here, Craig held the questions of the politics and form of community theatre works more open, but decisively invoked the 'network', a trope at the conceptual heart of the post-industrial 'network society' theorised by Manuel Castells and others from the 1990s onward, and in which contemporary community and applied theatre practice is without question implicated.[9] The Bubble's history reveals aspects of the broad genesis of 'community theatre' and the tensions it carries *vis à vis* other scenes of theatre practice and policy. It also raises questions as to the forces that have influenced this company's particular process of formation, now subsisting in a London that has completely transformed.

To identify London Bubble's current treatment of 'community', this article's case study explores *Blackbirds* (2011), a documentary piece created with participants of all ages about south Londoners' experience of the Blitz. Made in and for

---

[6]Ibid., p. 174.
[7]Sandy Craig, *Dreams and Deconstructions: Alternative Theatre in Britain*, ed. Sandy Craig (Ambergate: Amber Lane Press, 1980), p. 23.
[8]Ibid., p. 22.
[9]See George Yúdice, *The Expediency of Culture: Uses of Culture in the Global Era* (Durham, NC: Duke University Press, 2003) for an account of the network and its uses in the managerialisation of cultural work in the United States and Europe.

LONDON BOROUGH OF CAMDEN

THE BUBBLE THEATRE COMES TO TOWN!

With The London Blitz Show The Double Bubble for Kids & The Triple-Bill Bubble Show

at 8 pm

THE BLITZ SHOW

Wed. 30 August
Thur. 31 August
Sat. 2 September

THREE IN A BUBBLE

Fri. 1 September

FOR CHILDREN   at 2.30 pm

DOUBLE BUBBLE (Suitable for 4—10 year olds)

Wed. 30 August to Sat. 2 September

at KILBURN GRANGE PARK

Messina Avenue NW6

Admission: Evening 10p (OAP's 5p)   Children's Shows 2p

realise how starved parts of this city must be for live
professional theatre. In King George's Park, Wandsworth, last
Thursday the tent was full, and the local audience, all ages
from two to seventy, were alternately spellbound and noisily
involved. What they saw was a piece of episodic, half —

FIGURE 14 *Poster for* The Blitz Show *(1972), Bubble Theatre Company's first production. London Bubble Archive.*

a 'particular locality', *Blackbirds* amply fulfils Craig's criteria for 'community theatre'. It also provides a point of historical comparison. For, as creative director Jonathan Petherbridge announced to readers of *Blackbirds*' programme: 'On 1 May 1972, the newly formed Bubble Theatre Company opened their first ever production – *The Blitz Show*.'[10] Notionally set in an air-raid shelter, *The Blitz Show* aimed to 'recreate the feel and content of an evening of entertainments laid on by the Home Guard and the Women's Auxiliary'.[11] Nearly forty years later, *Blackbirds* used documentary techniques to acquaint members of a generation lacking immediate experience of the Blitz with older people who carried it 'in living memory', nostalgically citing a time 'when Britain was at its bravest and bombs fell daily in our streets'.[12]

Both productions thus engaged with one of the most ideologically freighted events of the history of twentieth century Britain. As historian Juliet Gardiner puts it:

The blitz has given the British – politicians in particular – a storehouse of images on which to draw in times of crisis: the symbol of an indomitable nation, united in resolution [...] The words that best sum up the blitz are probably 'endurance' and 'defiance'. And arising out of that, a sense of entitlement: that a nation that had been exhorted to 'take it' could reasonably expect, when the war was finally over, to 'get [some] of it', in terms of greater equality, more employment, better housing, education and life chances in general.[13]

---

[10] *Blackbirds* programme.

[11] 'Time Out', quoted in Rowlands, *Castles in the Park*, pp. 7–8.

[12] Simon Startin, 'Foreword', *Blackbirds: Inspired by South Londoners, Developed by Jonathan Petherbridge, and Written by Simon Startin* (Twickenham: Aurora Metro Publications, 2011), p. 9.

[13] Juliet Gardiner, *The Blitz: The British Under Attack* (London: Harper Press, 2010), p. xv. Simon Startin writes that *Blackbirds* is 'indebted' (2011, p. 9) to Gardiner's text.

One image taken out of the 'storehouse' in the 2000s was the 'Keep Calm and Carry On' poster. Created first in 1939 but never then actually seen by the general public, it is now a consumer craze imbued with meanings associated with the financial crisis and government-imposed anti-welfare 'austerity'.[14] It was, of course, the post-war Welfare State that enabled the Bubble and many other alternative theatre companies to be brought into being. Though far from comprehensive, this essay historicises the Bubble's emergence and development, and offers a close reading of *Blackbirds*, a piece responding to an area of south-east London on which the social and material changes of the twentieth century are starkly written.

'A new itinerant theatre company': The Bubble Theatre emerges

Unlike companies like Hull Truck, initiated by Mike Bradwell with an ad in *Time Out*, or Brighton Combination, whose first home was a Victorian school building taken over by Noel Greig, Ruth Marks and Jenny Harris, the Bubble Theatre was not initially the invention of artists. It was conceived by a funder – Greater London Arts Association (GLAA). GLAA had itself been established in 1966 to help enact transformation to London as a scene of cultural production. As an early GLAA annual report thundered polemically:

> Central London is considered the artistic centre of the world BUT MANY AREAS IN THE OUTER LONDON BOROUGHS ARE CULTURAL DESERTS AS DEVOID OF THE INCENTIVE FOR ARTISTIC ACTIVITY AND

---

[14] John Henley, 'What crisis? It's the Pin-up of Our Age, Gracing Homes, Shops – Even a US Embassy. Jon Henley on the Poster We Just Can't Stop Buying', *The Guardian*, 18 March 2009.

APPRECIATION AS THE MOST BACKWARD AREAS IN
THE REMOTEST PARTS OF THE UNITED KINGDOM.
THEIR VERY ENVIRONMENT MILITATES AGAINST
THE ARTS. [original emphasis][15]

The metropolitan elitism of this particular passage's tone
belies GLAA's gentler statements, and its enthusiastic support
of professional, amateur and educational arts initiatives
across the city, informed by the prevailing policy of extending
access to the arts as both a civic entitlement and a technique
of social integration.[16] And in 1970, GLAA's Drama Advisory
Panel (set up in the same year) announced its intention to
form 'a new itinerant theatre company specifically for touring
the London boroughs. It is hoped that this imaginative
new scheme could provide drama for the boroughs on a
permanent basis'.[17]

Imagining London as a vast, but dysfunctional, scene of
cultural resources, the same document expressed GLAA's hope
that

a specially designed portable building will not only appeal
to a far greater section of the population by breaking
down the traditional formal approach to the theatre,
but will also engender enthusiasm for the construction
of more flexible theatres and arts centres in the London
boroughs.[18]

---

[15] 'Greater London Arts Association Annual Report June 1969–July 1970' in
*The Greater London Arts Association Annual Report 1969/70 and Yearbook
for 1970/71* (London: Greater London Arts Association, 1970), p. 6.

[16] Franco Bianchini, 'GLC R.I.P.: Cultural Policies in London, 1981–1986',
New Formations 1 (1987), pp. 103–17, 104.

[17] 'Annual Report for 1st July 1970 to 31st August 1971: Drama and Dance'
in *The Greater London Arts Association Annual Report 1969/70 and
Yearbook for 1970/71*, p. 15.

[18] 'Annual Report for 1st July 1970 to 31st August 1971: Drama and Dance',
p. 15.

But according to the Bubble's first artistic director, Glen Walford, the idea for a touring theatre company had come first and that of a 'portable building' second. Invited to meet with GLAA to discuss running the project, Royal Court assistant director Walford had been 'an extremely reluctant pioneer of Bubble':[19]

> I said to them, 'No way, I'm fed up of going into draughty halls and having caretakers ... I've done it' – because I had, I'd already done it in Sheffield. And Peter [James, Young Vic Associate Director, and member of GLAA working party] said 'Well, just come and talk to them ...' So I did. And of course, when you don't really want a job, you can be sure as hell that you're going to get it. So I was in this room with all these quite impressive people who were gathered together, God knows why, and I was saying, 'Well, hmmm ...' And then somebody said 'Well, what would make you do it?' ... I was actually answering the question of myself. 'What would make me want to do it is if you had this wonderful structure that was ... like a sort of bubble – you floated into a park, you landed there, and at the end of the week it all went away.'[20]

The 'bubble' eventually to be designed was a custom-built mobile polyhedral tent with solid sides and a canvas roof, accommodating a hundred audience members.

Supported by an assistant, Walford then undertook a year of research and liaison with the boroughs. She refused to confine the company to 'the likes of Edmonton and Enfield',[21] instead also strategically negotiating spots in 'key places like Highbury Fields and Blackheath, where you know that the people in the

---

[19] 'Bubble's Mavericks and Groundbreakers', http://www.youtube.com/watch?v=kcV0wf9bsEM (accessed August 2012).
[20] Interview with Glen Walford, September 2011.
[21] Ibid.

know are going to come and spread the word'.[22] Reflecting her commercial acuity and feel for glitz, she called the Bubble's ramshackle base, a garage conversion in Kentish Town, 'The Roxy'. The artistic work was inspired, meanwhile, by the early modern trope of travelling 'rogues and vagabonds'.[23] Walford intended to provide music-based theatre with a sense of 'mischief'[24] to non-theatregoing audiences, setting great store by 'the air of decadence, and originality of course, you know – this mad tent could be offering something that they had no experience of whatsoever'.[25] The company's first main stage piece, *The Blitz Show* (1972–3), was made in the style of music hall, devised using research assembled by writer Frank Hatherley and worked into a script to be played in-the-round. In his enthusiastic review, *The Guardian*'s Michael Billington summarised the piece as 'a jolly Joan Littlewoodish concoction of songs and sketches supposedly staged in an air-raid shelter by a group of bomb-scarred Londoners'.[26] John Peter of *The Sunday Times* approvingly acknowledged the presence of a 'local audience, all ages from 2 to 70 [who] were alternately spellbound and noisily involved'.[27] Yet Billington's review also reflects the ambivalence of the terms of the Bubble's projected engagement with audiences. Rehearsing GLAA's own rhetoric, Billington referred to the desirability of 'rapid cultural decentralization'[28] and a top-down, quasi-evangelical process of 'spreading theatre among people'.[29] Meanwhile, *Time Out*'s reviewer gave the piece and its politics short shrift. According to the then-radical magazine, founded in London in 1968 and

---

[22] Ibid.
[23] Ibid.
[24] Ibid.
[25] Ibid.
[26] Michael Billington, 'The Blitz Show at the Bubble Theatre', *The Guardian*, 2 May 1972.
[27] John Peter. Quoted in Rowlands, *Castles in the Park*, p. 7.
[28] Billington, 'The Blitz Show'.
[29] Ibid.

pivotal to the flourishing alternative theatre movement,[30] *The Blitz Show*'s 'loose cheery evocation of the happy together spirit of the war, put over through songs, dances, sketches, competitions' offered nothing more than 'sentiment, sentiment all the way, with not a bite in it'.[31] The critic demanded: 'Is the Blitz the only unifying factor in "deprived areas"? That's hard to take.'[32] This position resonates with later critiques, by writers like Angus Calder and Paul Gilroy, of the ideological content of Second World War nostalgia.[33]

While the Bubble certainly produced a government-sponsored version of Littlewood's 'popular community theatre',[34] it did not explicitly promote a socialist politics. It is telling that the company does not appear in Catherine Itzin's compendious *Stages in the Revolution* (1980) alongside other groups of the period. Writing in 1985, Tony Rowlands insisted that the Bubble's 'message, in the biblical sense, is universal; groundlings and nobs can co-exist. The Shakespearean Globe was "the glory of the (South) bank": the Bubble Theatre's unique contribution is to be a mobile glory of everywhere.'[35] Yet the Bubble did not shrink from satirizing itself and its methods of attracting 'non-traditional audiences'. The insert for a promotional LP of songs performed in *The Blitz Show*, distributed for the show's revival in 1973, impudently speaks truth to power:

> How had the Bubble arrived? Well, that's a long story. Briefly, an intelligence organization called GLAA under the sinister Commander H. West OBE, wanted a mobile

---

[30] Craig, *Dreams and Deconstructions*, p. 16.

[31] 'The Bubble Theatre, Hackney', *Time Out*, 5–11 May 1972, p. 29.

[32] Ibid.

[33] Angus Calder, *The Myth of the Blitz* (London: Pimlico, 1992); Paul Gilroy, *After Empire: Melancholia or Convivial Culture?* (Abingdon and New York: Routledge, 2004).

[34] Catherine Itzin, *Stages in the Revolution: Political Theatre in Britain since 1968* (London: Methuen, 1980), p. 5.

[35] Rowlands, *Castles in the Sky*, p. 10.

propaganda unit dedicated to saying that getting high on art is infinitely better than continually putting in pay claims ... Operation 'Arts for the Plebs' got off the ground. Basically, the first idea was to trap the plebs inside a tent within a pitch-dark park or open space in some remote area of London as far as possible for any means of transport. As part of the softening-up process absolutely no paths were lighted and the tent placed as far away as possible from any road and near to a pond. Thus, the eager-beaver pleb was given a sense of achievement when actually stumbling against the theatre. A brilliant psychological point this, running counter to the Wesker/Berman school which aims to make art for the masses easily available.[36]

Clearly the company was confident that the work they were producing did not remotely approach its audience members as unthinking 'plebs', but as people able to understand a joke, and its intended target, when they saw it.

The Bubble I came to know as a staff member in the 2000s looked very different from the Bubble of the 1970s. Its complex programme featured large-scale outdoor promenade (a form introduced to the company by Petherbridge), site-specific work in non-theatre spaces and topical, cleverly told Christmas pantomimes in theatres. It produced smaller-scale education and participatory projects in schools, youth clubs and community centres, frequently on the model of 'peer-group education'. In 1990, it became one of the first companies in Britain to engage with the work of Augusto Boal; a project entitled *Lost Histories* (1989), made by the Bubble's associate director Adrian Jackson with travelling communities, and, subsequently, theatre projects using Boal's methods, were the beginning of Cardboard Citizens, the homeless people's theatre company of which Jackson is now artistic director.[37]

---

[36] 'The Best of Bubble', LP insert, from Glen Walford's personal archive.
[37] Interview with Jonathan Petherbridge.

In the late 1990s, the work of American educationalist Vivian Gussin Paley inspired theatre projects with the early years, which Trisha Lee, former participatory projects director, continues to make with her company Makebelieve Arts. Together, its projects articulated the company's fundamental understanding of theatre as 'an inherently social artform'.[38] The company's history was seldom discussed, and I assumed that its roots were to be found in the theatre-in-education and animateur movements of the 1970s.[39] The narrative above shows that this was far from accurate. So, how did the Bubble of the 1990s and 2000s come into being?

'More closely linked with the community': The Bubble in the 1980s

The company's turn to participatory practice dates from a moment of crisis in the 1980s, when, at the behest of GLAA, the company was partially re-imagined in terms of 'community action'. Despite successes – including then-artistic director Bob Carlton's Olivier Award-winning *Return to the Forbidden Planet* (1983), a science fiction musical adaptation of *The Tempest* that became a global smash hit – in 1983, GLAA threatened to remove its grant entirely. In a leader article in *The Stage*, the company's administrator Sarah Holmes declared 'we just don't understand it – all we've heard is some criticism about our shows not being political but we're here to entertain not educate'.[40] Following energetic lobbying, it was finally agreed that GLAA would restrict its

---

[38] Susan Smillie, 'Case study: London Bubble', *The Observer*, 13 January 2008.

[39] Tony Coult, 'Agents of the Future' in Craig (ed.), *Dreams and Deconstructions*, pp. 76–85.

[40] Angela Thomas, 'Fears Grow for GLAA Cash as Bubble Faces Axe', *The Stage*, 25 August 1983, p. 1.

subsidy to fifty per cent of the total, pushing the company to seek more funds from the London boroughs and other sources, in unmistakable alignment with the demands of Thatcherite cultural policy.[41] And, as part of this programme of change, GLAA and the Bubble 'reached agreement that Bubble's future should be more closely linked with the community'.[42]

At 'Return to the Forbidden Elephant', an evening of discussion about London Bubble in the 1980s held at the Bubble in autumn 2012, Sarah Holmes, speaking alongside Bob Carlton, Bob Eaton and Peter Rowe (artistic directors during the 1980s), recalled that GLAA had stipulated that for the Bubble simply to produce plays was no longer sufficient. Instead, it must begin to produce what were known in the shorthand of the time as 'tower block shows' for audiences in economically deprived areas. According to Carlton, on hearing of this turn of events, Glen Walford urged he and the company 'to keep it colourful, and not to do a tower block show – because the last thing people need is middle class people coming and telling them about their lives'. Despite its limited experience in the area, the company embraced the challenge to make community work wholeheartedly, seeking advice from colleagues like Jude Kelly (then at Battersea Arts Centre) as to the appropriate methods. Director Rob Swain (then a stage manager for the company) recalls a period of training, led by artists including Walford, Ken Campbell, Claire Venables and Willy Russell, staged in preparation for the summer season of 1985–6.[43] Later, a 'projects team' was introduced, creating community projects to run concurrently with the shows playing in repertory in the tent, now performed by an 'integrated' company of actors. And in

---

[41] Kate Dorney and Ros Merkin, 'Introduction' in *The Glory of the Garden: English Regional Theatre and the Arts Council 1984–2009* (Newcastle upon Tyne: Cambridge Scholars Publishing, 2010), pp. 1–14, 5–7.

[42] Anon, 'Bubble Future is Brighter', *The Stage*, 27 October 1983.

[43] Interview with Rob Swain, July 2011.

1987, the company moved its base from Kentish Town to Rotherhithe on the banks of the Thames, adjacent to London's Docklands, an area undergoing aggressive governmental intervention to create a new industrial site for the financial services. Peter Rowe described how, in that moment in the late 1980s, the Bubble's new base on Elephant Lane, SE16 became connected in the minds of local people with gentrification, even though the company was 'trying to work with people resisting that change' – part of which took the form of the production of a show entitled *I Fought Yuppie Zombies from Hell* (1988).

These transformations were by no means easy. Touring to Millwall Park in 1985, black company members were subjected to racist abuse from audiences, and refused to continue;[44] on another occasion, the National Front daubed the tent with graffiti.[45] Controversy and antagonism of a different order was experienced within the company, its focus the perceived asymmetry of importance between 'shows' and 'education'. Jonathan Petherbridge – appointed artistic director in 1989 – says of this moment that 'they grafted on to what essentially was a performance-based community theatre company a participatory team, and it always felt like a graft, until we changed the way the company operated'[46] – which is to say, by creating more dialogue between the strands of the company, researching and experimenting with participatory methodologies for work with children and young people, and decommissioning the tent to make greater resources available for work beyond its summer season.

---

[44] Ibid.

[45] 'Return to the Forbidden Elephant', 29 September 2012.

[46] Jonathan Petherbridge interview.

Case study: *Grandchildren of the Blitz* and *Blackbirds*

The Bubble's early work encompassed 'community' in terms of 'the popular' and 'suburban'. From the 1980s onward, it became aligned with an ideology of what George Yúdice calls 'culture-as-resource',[47] which reframes cultural production as a mechanism for economic and social development. Though more explicit in the Thatcherite 1980s, a version of this ideology arguably underpinned the initial formation of the company by GLAA. Moving now to the 2010s, and this essay's main case study, we can see many of these concepts – 'popular', 'socially-engaged', 'participation' – reflected in London Bubble's documentary theatre work *Blackbirds* (2011), 'a play emerging from a year of intergenerational conversations about the effects of the Blitz on London and Londoners'.[48] This programme byline elegantly summarises a complex project – in fact, two projects addressing London Bubble's south London neighbourhood. The first, an oral history project called *Grandchildren of the Blitz*, assembled two groups of people as 'interviewers' and 'interviewees' – children and young people between the ages of eight and seventeen, and older people, some in their eighties and nineties, who had themselves survived the Blitz. Petherbridge commeted:

> The people we were talking to were children themselves during the war. I find that quite difficult to absorb, strangely. And while my generation, I think, know quite a lot about it, and were slightly attuned to it because of the effect it had on our parents – not to say that our parents talked about it, but it really affected their lives – I'm not

---

[47] George Yúdice, *The Expediency of Culture*, p. 1.
[48] *Blackbirds* programme.

sure the younger generations or the generations that have come after are attuned in that way, and therefore it was a direct attempt to attune them to that – but also, to bring those generations together to have a conversation about it. I thought it was a way of peeling back a layer effectively.[49]

The project was thus in part imagined as an educative, even socially therapeutic, process, as much as an historical and theatrical one. Along with archival research at the Imperial War Museum and Southwark Local History Library, the findings of the interviews would become a resource for theatre-making. The result was *Blackbirds*, a performance whose two short tours to venues in the area were attended, in sum, by more than one and a half thousand people.

Grandchildren of the Blitz

Grandchildren of the Blitz approached 'history' as a process of enquiry encompassing action in the present. Training as fledgling oral historians in the summer of 2010, members of the group of twenty-four young interviewers first visited London's Imperial War Museum.[50] They participated in workshops inviting imaginative reflection upon the wartime experiences of similarly aged young people, through handling objects (gas and 'baby' gas masks) and exploring newspaper clippings and 'profiles' of evacuees from the city. Having begun a process of asking, of the children of 1940s London, 'what they'd be thinking and what they'd be going through', project leader

---

[49] Interview with Marigold Hughes, Shipra Ogra and Jonathan Petherbridge, July 2011.
[50] 'Meet the Gatherers', http://www.grandchildrenoftheblitz.com/meet-the-gatherers.aspx (accessed August 2012). Many of *Grandchildren of the Blitz*'s twenty-four young interviewers were already members of London Bubble's youth theatre groups, while others chose to participate following project leader Marigold Hughes' offer of taster workshops to schools in the Southwark area.

Marigold Hughes then staged a series of workshops at the Bubble, which took the young interviewers' understanding of the historical situation as the starting point.[51]

> At the beginning of the whole process ... I said to the young people: 'What do you want to know about the Blitz, and what do you think you don't know?' We made a whole 'brainstorm' about it, and then I structured the programme of training around all those things that they wanted to know.[52]

Hughes invited Neil Bright, a local historian, to present an account of the docks' implication in the Blitz, and specifically the area around Rotherhithe. Bright took the participants on a 'Blitz walk', enabling the participants to begin to make associations between the events described and their own lived experience. Next, the group – consisting now of the young people and a group of adult volunteers – received interview training from an oral historian from the British Library. Reflecting semi-structured interview methodologies widely practised by sociologists and historians, the young people were advised to devise open questions dealing with broad topics – 'rations, games, bombing, family, evacuation'[53] – to allow the interviewees to speak freely, encouraged to imagine the interview as a 'tree' with a number of 'branches' of questioning. This metaphor reflects *Grandchildren of the Blitz*'s own structure, in which many contributed on its peripheries, while others ultimately became its 'trunk'.

Fifteen older interviewees came forward in response to local press advertising and workshops staged in day centres and sheltered accommodation units. Incorporating conversation about photographs, maps and so on, Hughes felt that

---

[51] Marigold Hughes interview.
[52] Ibid.
[53] Ibid.

these workshops, in which around a hundred older people participated, 'almost turned into more informal interviews, [and] very naturally led into a discussion of people's experiences'.[54] Some were reluctant to participate in *Grandchildren of the Blitz* itself but embraced the opportunity to speak in the workshops.

> There was a lady called Annie who was blind, and couldn't actually see the photo, but she said when she was little, she was on her way home, and she saw a fighter plane come so low that she could see the swastika and see the pilot's face. And that she knocked on the nearest door and got swept in there and was fine. But really, I think as soon as you unleash that subject, people have got such strong memories of it – and generally, I think the consensus was with everyone, that they just don't talk about it anymore. No one talks about it, in the same way that we don't talk about it, or when we get to that age, we don't talk about our childhoods.[55]

Inviting young people to act as the project's primary researching interviewers of course gently questioned the processes by which social history ordinarily comes to be written, and by whom. Added to this, their questions of the interviewees revealed the interview processes themselves to possess a certain kind of theatricality:

> There were things that we wouldn't even think about asking about that a ten year old would. There was a moment when Edward, who was one of our interviewers, said to Barbara: 'Oh Barbara, when the bombs were coming down and you were in the air raid shelter, did you ever just think about cutting a little hole in the roof and peering out so you could

---

[54] Ibid.
[55] Ibid.

see all the bombs falling?' ... I think there are things that to our point of view, we look back and think 'wasn't it terrible, wasn't it horrible', and obviously for them, if they went through it now ... [but] they're at the point where their lives are just a playful adventure, so that's the lens that they see that time through, so I think a lot of their questions were about games and toys.[56]

Though we might question the normative construct of childhood as 'play' that emerges in these reflections – and, of course, not all the interviewers were children – they offer a powerful sense of the interviews as invitations to the older people revisit their pasts, prompted, in part, by the young people's own exercise of imagination in relation to their own present identities.

Blackbirds

Blackbirds was produced, in part, in response to the resulting interview texts. Participants and artists made the piece together over the course of several months, in a process that characteristically saw many participants drop in and out before a final, multigenerational company of thirty-eight performers was assembled. Young people and adults worked alongside one another, including some – for example, Robert and Kezia Herzog – who were parent and child. The creation of the piece consisted of three phases – an effort, in autumn 2010, to transform the interview texts into theatrical material, and in spring 2011, the writing and designing of the show on the basis of the emerging work of the group, and then rehearsal of the written piece, documented eventually by a published script. The premise of the piece was simply to tell 'the story of what happened to Mayflower Street in Bermondsey'.[57]

---

[56] Ibid.
[57] Jonathan Petherbridge interview.

Director Jonathan Petherbridge's reflections on the process echo those of other contemporary theatre-makers both in regard to the onerous nature of producing the interview 'documents' themselves and storytelling:

> The autumn term, the actual work, trying out material, was very difficult. And it was difficult because that is a difficult task to set yourself, inherently, because those stories are so dramatic and singular, and turning them into something that was collaborative, and is better than the person just describing it ... you know, does it *need* theatre?[58]

In the script's preface, writer Simon Startin's framing of the interviewees' words as 'having more authenticity than anything I could concoct'[59] is not quite of the same order as Petherbridge's assessment of the stories' inherent 'drama'. But, in its commitment to a kind of collective authorship, and an effort, as Startin puts it, to offer an impressionistic sense of 'the spirit of that time',[60] *Blackbirds'* working process involved a mix of techniques which did not in fact fetishise the interviewees as wellspring of documentary authenticity. Instead, the project used documentary techniques to access a particular 'truth' about the social and material experience of the Blitz – which, though underscored by a logic of realism, might also be expressed through non-realist theatrical representation.

The process was first structured around 'tasks' prompted by documentary sources. Petherbridge says:

> We did a number of experiments. And some of those were scripted experiments. Sometimes it was taking inter-views and editing interviews in order to use certain parts,

---

[58] Ibid.
[59] Startin, *Blackbirds*, p. 9.
[60] Ibid.

FIGURE 15 Blackbirds, *Dilston Grove, London (2011). Photo: Steve Hickey.*

sometimes it was taking facts. We spent an evening going: 'what's an interesting way in which to impart to an audience the number of bombs that were dropped on London?' ... 'What's a different way to do a radio interview, something coming off the radio?' So we set ourselves tasks. And then he [Startin] would come in, and look at what we had done, and try to include the ones that worked.[61]

Startin's 'brief' was, straightforwardly, to 'be imagistic, write whatever you want to write'.[62] This resulted in an iterative process of devising, writerly 'feedback' (as it were), and further devising. For example, Startin's introduction of a group of women carrying tea became the prompt for a fragment in which sugar lumps, dropped into crockery, would represent bombs falling on the city. The process of creation was time and labour intensive, and often 'really hard. But there were moments, just occasional moments of: "that is fantastic. That is just gorgeous. If we can get that level of concentration and intensity this will work" – but it took hours to get that ten seconds.'[63]

Reflecting this idea of incremental production, woven through the process were multiple moments of re-enactment – in the sense, as Rebecca Schneider puts it, of 're-playing or re-doing a precedent event, artwork or act'.[64] From winter 2010, 'Make Do and Mend', a series of additional drop-in practical workshops initiated by designer Pip Nash, allowed participants to engage in activities related to the period. The first workshop anticipated Christmas: everyone made decorative paper-chains, gesturing towards and re-enacting wartime preparations for seasonal festivity. Hughes felt that this first workshop succeeded in providing a space for the

---

[61] Jonathan Petherbridge interview.

[62] Ibid.

[63] Ibid.

[64] Rebecca Schneider, *Performing Remains: Art and War in Times of Theatrical Re-enactment* (London and New York: Routledge, 2011), p. 2.

older interviewees to continue to participate in the project and 'to tell us a bit about the food, or the hairstyles, or whatever',[65] and in creating an easy-going environment for conversation between participants, young and old:

When your hands are busy, people are much more relaxed about talking. And I think there's definitely a sense that though 'we're all making our separate things', they were making something together, and I think that really opens people up, and you feel like – I think it's something about you doing something on very equal terms, there's no hierarchy, everyone's doing the same thing.[66]

In their exploration of sheltering, the company attempted the impossible task of approximating, in rehearsal, the nightly wartime experience of retreating from the falling bombs, taping out a 'life-size' area on the rehearsal room floor and experimenting with physically inhabiting it. Taking their lead from the interviewees' descriptions of cramming into highly confined spaces for protection, the company's theatrical re-enactments were then juxtaposed with those texts, spoken aloud in performance. As Petherbridge describes, this involved 'going into detail, and replaying it physically against [the words of the] people who were actually describing it, who did it' – an act engaging both 'the witness, and the replay'.[67] The older interviewees – here conceived as 'witnesses' – would then also be invited into the rehearsal room.

When David or Brenda or whomever would come in and watch it, they would critique it – they'd sort of go 'that's right', or 'that's not right', or 'you're missing out an important detail' … And you felt when they watched …

---

[65] Jonathan Petherbridge interview.
[66] Marigold Hughes interview.
[67] Jonathan Petherbridge interview.

you got this sense of – some bell was being rung, something was being sounded in the person. And that affected me, it affected me and Jools [Julia Voce, assistant director] – I've never cried in rehearsals as much as we cried. When we hit something and got it right ... You know, often, you didn't, but five minutes in every two weeks, you'd actually get something right. And you felt in some way that it was – cathartic is too strong a word, but it's along those lines.[68]

Here, there is something of the order of Schneider's notion that 'any approach to history involving remains – material *or* immaterial remains – engages temporality at (and as) chiasm, where times cross and, in crossing, in some way touch'.[69] Informed by theorists of culture likewise interested in theorising 'feeling', Schneider speaks of 'the jump and the touch of affect',[70] an entity 'bearing atmosphere-altering tendencies, in material remains or in gestic/ritual remains, carried in a sentence or a song, shifting in and through bodies in encounter'[71] such as those gathered in London Bubble's rehearsal room, trying to re-imagine the events of the Blitz.

Other elements of the process likewise hybridised the exercise of theatrical imagination and attention to documentary source. *Blackbirds'* dramatic action involved 'no entrances or exits; all performers work on stage at all times and the theatre language is that of an ensemble rather than individual star turns'.[72] But the ensemble was not simply massed on stage, but organised into a series of smaller theatrical units – the households of Mayflower Street. At the beginning of the piece, the stage would be completely bare; when the company entered, they would bring a vast array of objects, with which they lined the stage, producing a loose and crowded sense of a series of

---

[68] Ibid.
[69] Schneider, *Performing Remains*, p. 37.
[70] Ibid., p. 36.
[71] Ibid., p. 36.
[72] Startin, *Blackbirds*, pp. 8–9.

dwellings occupied by 'families'. Their design emerged from theatrical experiment:

> We put them [the 'families'] together randomly, almost, into a 'house' – and it was pretty random. They then do a bit of the research, then the designer comes along, and the director, and the lighting designer, and say: 'Tell us about your house.' And they, in a way, designed what came back to them.[73]

Though the design team led this process, this strategy is Stanislavskyan in its solicitation of the participants' thoughts about the 'real' circumstances of the 'homes' they would occupy, on stage, for the duration of the performance. The performers would remain in character throughout, engaging in everyday activities (cleaning objects, reading, and so on) to provide what Hughes – who performed in the piece several times – called a 'throughline', allowing individuals, as members of 'families', to 'map [their] way through the years'.[74] A naturalistic ethic of practice is reflected, too, in directorial preparations toward the enactment of the fate of Mayflower Street's residents.

> We did not tell the inhabitants of Mayflower Street the end of their story for a very, very long time. Deliberately. We did loads and loads of stuff about the houses, about the smells of their houses, about their front doors, about interactions, about the transitions between the houses, and I held it, deliberately held it back for a long, long time.[75]

The penultimate gesture of the piece would be the departure from the stage of the families whose homes were destroyed, a gentle but awful signifier of their deaths. For Hughes, seeing this staged for the first time was among the most emotive

---

[73] Jonathan Petherbridge interview.
[74] Marigold Hughes interview.
[75] Jonathan Petherbridge interview.

moments in the devising process, bringing 'the scale of the violence and deaths to a very personal level [...] when you can tie it down to one family, and to one street, and to a child and an adult, and a father and a mother and a son'.[76]

Created using this bricolage of techniques, the resulting performance work was often captivating. I attended the performance twice during its run at Dilston Grove (formerly Clare College Mission Church, built in 1912) in Southwark Park, SE16. The concrete-constructed space possesses a very high ceiling, imposing windows which allow scant light inside, and at one end, a slightly raised end-on platform which functioned as the stage for *Blackbirds*' action. Sitting in the packed audience in this expansive, cavernous space, on one of the fold-up chairs arranged in rows facing the stage, the walls carried a slight smell of damp – anticipating the sensation of being underground which the play would partially dramatise. Petherbridge characterised *Blackbirds* as:

> unusual for the new Bubble because it is inspired not by the present, but an echo, by an absence – and a living memory. Usually we work from contemporary surroundings and references. *Blackbirds* refers to buildings that no longer stand, to an industry that is long gone, to people who were killed in houses and shelters that stood beside the streets we walk or ride along today.[77]

Blackbirds attempted to embody the paradox that is 'living memory'. The play described a linear temporal trajectory – the beginning of the war, to the end of the terror of the Blitz. But, like the scenographic arrangement of the households and their occupants around the stage, Startin pursued this trajectory carefully through thematic 'units' of action (evacuation, administration, entertainment) which problematised that

---

[76] Marigold Hughes interview.
[77] *Blackbirds* programme.

sense of linearity. Each unit comprised storytelling from the piece's fictional characters, moments of recorded speech from the interviewees, and narration of historical data drawn from documentary sources. The play's collage-like structure thus corroborated Derek Paget's assessment that documentary theatre is most often an anti-naturalistic 'theatre of interruption',[78] while also showing, as he remarks of Theatre Workshop's *Oh! What a Lovely War* (1963), that naturalism 'could be part of the methodological mix' of documentary works.[79]

The wartime world the play portrayed was bookended, narratively, by moments from the present – reflecting the hoped-for 'peeling back' of a layer of time of *Grandchildren of the Blitz*. The play opened with a segment more symbolic than naturalistic: a dialogue between an older woman, and a young girl – in the script called, simply, 'Elder' and 'Younger'. Mounting the stage from the front, they climbed up a set of steps positioned in the middle before coming to a stop and readying themselves to speak. Entirely empty, the bare stage consolidated the brittle effect of their peremptory statements:

E: You're very young.
Y: You're very old.
E: You make too much noise.
Y: You're very grumpy.[80]

The full exchange, dealing in stereotype and superficial appearance, concluded with the promise from 'Elder' to speak of her life 'before the sun goes down',[81] suggesting the

---

[78] Derek Paget, 'The "Broken Tradition" and its Continued Powers of Endurance', in Alison Forsyth and Chris Megson (eds), *Get Real: Documentary Theatre Past and Present* (Basingstoke: Palgrave Macmillan, 2009), pp. 224–38, p. 229.
[79] Ibid.
[80] Startin, *Blackbirds*, p. 17.
[81] Ibid.

forthcoming piece, in part, to have the consciousness-raising agenda of refuting those stereotypes. Shifting to a bluer, more clinical lighting state, the stage rapidly became a branch of Tesco, where company members – whose contemporary costume largely concealed the floral prints and 1940s suits worn beneath – shopped with wire baskets in imaginary aisles, while another enacted 'scanning' to a familiar automated 'boop' sound-effect. 'Younger' now stood, downstage left, with a boy. She held aloft a length of white cloth, on to which was projected the filmed image of an older man, speaking to the boy about the docks that formerly occupied this site: 'Yes. This very spot. Where that counter is, there was a crane. And I'd be standing here, with my mate, who's dead now.'[82] This 'Tesco' was pointing, theatrically, toward a real Tesco, situated moments away from Dilston Grove, in the place now called Surrey Quays. The old man's speech became interwoven with other company members' direct narrative address – '"And we asked questions. They were children during the Blitz." / "Ships and cranes and crates and boxes from all over the British Empire. It was called Surrey Docks then."'[83] – heralding a brisk transition from the present 'Tesco' to the 'Mayflower Street' of the past. The performers on the stage removed their modern clothing, the baskets were disappeared, and a great horde of other performers filed purposefully on to the stage. The jumbled collocation of wooden furniture, standard lamps, objects and fabric they brought, over which hung a series of large paper sculptures – garments, speaking of barrage balloons and things 'unused – dresses that have been left by dead people'[84] – was the world we would watch for the majority of the performance.

Throughout, *Blackbirds* treated audio-visual documents as revenants – ghosts from a now-inaccessible past – in present

---

[82] Ibid., p. 18.

[83] Ibid.

[84] Jonathan Petherbridge interview.

FIGURE 16 Blackbirds, *Dilston Grove, London (2011)*. *Photo: Steve Hickey.*

dialogue with live action. Early in the piece, the residents of 'Mayflower Street No. 11' fearfully assembled 'round the wireless'[85] to listen to Chamberlain's announcement that the country was at war – a beautifully staged recording of the real broadcast which resounded uncannily around the walls of the church like a despatch from the beyond. This technique, applied also to the recorded voices of the interviewees, circumvented any sense of reifying the older people and their words. Not presented as indexical of 'the past', these were conversations that had simply taken place in a more recent past, and were shown to be in a complex temporal relationship to other documents and the play's theatrical explorations. Nonetheless, *Blackbirds*' representations sometimes appeared anachronistic, at other times, nostalgic. 'Mayflower Street No. 8' provided the venue for an IKEA joke: father 'Ham', ineptly building an Anderson shelter, is told by daughter 'Rosie-Lea'

---

[85] Startin, *Blackbirds*, p. 22.

that he has 'got the instructions upside down'.[86] Draped with household accoutrements of the 1940s, the stage theatricalised the period, but also to an extent resembled the current décor of fashionable London café-bars, heavy with nostalgia for this earlier moment of austerity. However, any sense that the piece was attempting to provide uncritical comfort was instantly banished with the staging, halfway through, of 'Black Saturday', the aerial bombing of the docks. Verbal descriptions of the bombing of the factories along the river, theatrical exchanges between sheltering families, and the recorded words of the interviewees culminated in an unbearably long, bone-shudderingly loud sound of an explosion, while a red lighting effect ripped across the back of the darkened stage. The light illuminated the bodies of the sheltering performers, massed in a group, clutching one another for support. It produced a sense, persisting throughout the piece, of a populus being buffeted by forces that seemed utterly beyond their control, supported by the words of interviewee Gladys: 'I can't explain the feeling; there is nothing you can do. You can't run anywhere; you don't run out, you'd just do as you're told.'[87] With this moment, and the subsequent account of wartime governmental surveillance and management of morale, evoking David Cameron's reported desire to measure 'Gross National Happiness',[88] the piece appeared to offer a critique of twenty-first-century economic 'austerity'.

Conclusion

London Bubble has been a feature of the city's culture since 1972 in both its playful peregrinations across London and its later practice of participatory theatre-making in specific

---

[86] Ibid., p. 35.
[87] Ibid., p. 29.
[88] Allegra Stratton, 'Happiness Index to Gauge Britain's National Mood', *The Guardian*, 14 November 2010.

neighbourhoods. But London is now greatly changed. Its population is no longer declining, as it was in the 1970s, but booming. Old warehouses and factories are now luxury apartments, with art events frequently having eased the transition between the two for developers. Performance in non-theatre locations is no longer exceptional, but ubiquitous. And GLAA's intention, in 1970, that the Bubble would 'provide drama for the boroughs on a permanent basis'[89] is itself indicative of a long-disappeared political moment. For publicly funded artistic practice in the twenty-first century, a key directive is 'innovation'.

In 2008 London Bubble lost its status as an Arts Council RFO (Regularly Funded Organisation) as part of a highly controversial round of cuts – the first of those imposed in the wake of the financial crisis of 2007:

If the Bubble's appeals fail, the thirty-five–year-old company will close.

'There's a theme here, "old wood is dead wood",' says Petherbridge. 'The Arts Council feels we haven't reinvented ourselves but they haven't looked at two-thirds of our work. We are constantly questioning what we do and how we do it.'[90]

In 2008, the company also lost its substantial London Councils grant. Taken together, this represented around sixty-five per cent of its annual revenue, forcing the company into the position of making a number of its core staff redundant. The company did not close, but began to pursue philanthropic support more assertively, successfully negotiating a large, fixed-term donation from a wealthy supporter. It also conceived Fan Made Theatre, a model of fundraising and performance commissioning inviting audiences to act as

---

[89] Annual Report for 1st July 1970 to 31st August 1971: Drama and Dance, p. 15.
[90] Susan Smillie, 'Case Study: London Bubble'. *The Observer*, 13 January 2008.

'stakeholders' in the creation of artistic work – some time before 'crowd-funding' really took off in Britain.

Arguably consistently at the forefront of developments in its particular mode of practice, the Bubble has also taken a pragmatic political approach to the negotiation of its survival, a pragmatism thematised in *Blackbirds*. Though I read *Blackbirds* as offering a critique of austerity, the end of play features this exchange:

AMIE: What you looking at Mum?

RISI: The blackbirds. Up there. Building the nest on that chimney.

AMIE: But that house is bombed out.

RISI: Council gonna knock it down tomorrow. But them blackbirds don't know about tomorrow, do they?
They don't even know they are born. They just look after their family. There's peace with them. No war or bombs or all the rest of it.

AMIE: We should scare them off. It's not safe.

RISI: No ... let them have today. There's a lot more war to come.

MARY: *[recording] Let's hope that you never have to go through what I went through because you can have nice things and do what you want, do things that you want to do.* [emphasis in original][91]

Like *The Blitz Show*, this passage is saturated with ironic and implicit reference to the contemporary context, and does not urge audiences to protest.

Unlike the Bubble of 1972, the company is not only a temporary visitor to places across London. It is a fixture of a single neighbourhood, and an occasional visitor to others, borne out by these words from a participant:

---

[91] Startin, *Blackbirds*, pp. 48–9.

I was a London Bubble baby, before I was born. It has always been constant thing in my life, and has always been there for me, whatever is going on in my life. When I was seven my parents broke up, and a social worker took me to a workshop and I remember thinking: 'this is what I want to do'. My mother took me to the show that night, *Arabian Nights* – it was my first theatrical experience. If it wasn't for London Bubble I would not be where I am now – I would not have gone to university and studied theatre, and I thank my parents for being supportive ... People ask: 'how is it going at London Bubble', and it becomes engrained in your life, and it has etched onto other people in my life.[92]

In the 1970s, full funding from GLAA provided the conditions for the Bubble's theatrical travels. In the 2010s, we see GLAA's projected 'permanence' in another form. Alongside its touring theatre work, the Bubble offers the continuity of a welcoming and creative home to many people in a context that, in terms of the future of publicly funded arts work, as with other aspects of the welfare state, is far more uncertain.

[92] Alison Rooke and David Kendall, *Taking Part Case Study: London Bubble Theatre* (London: Centre for Urban and Community Research, Goldsmiths, University of London, 2012), p. 15.

9

Sue Emmas

Interview and introduction by Lily Einhorn

Sue Emmas started working at the Young Vic in 1991 and for the last ten years has been associate artistic director. During this time she has created and overseen a number of versions of the Taking Part department, moulding it into the three strands of which it consists at present: Schools and Colleges; Participation (young people ages eight to twenty-five outside of an educational setting) working in the Young Vic; and Two Boroughs – working with local residents and community groups from the boroughs of Lambeth and Southwark where the theatre is located. All of Taking Part's work is rooted in the Young Vic's neighbourhood, responding to a complex, diverse community and welcoming it into its theatre.

Community theatre companies often operate outside traditional theatre spaces. The Young Vic's participatory practice takes place within its own theatre building, inviting a diversity of groups to take part in its work. On average, Taking Part gives 10,000 free tickets a year to people of all ages, socio-economic backgrounds, ethnicities and cultures within Lambeth and Southwark, enabling them to see shows, take part in workshops and, from time to time, in productions. In essence, Taking Part aims to extend equality of opportunity to theatre – both as audiences and as makers. It operates with the simple idea that the more we all learn about the world and each other, the better off that world will be.

The department, originally known as TPR (Teaching, Participation and Research) was set up under Tim Supple's artistic direction in 1991. One key facet to the department's work was research into how best to connect with an audience. This connection took place in many ways, including the repeated offer of free tickets to local people, thereby creating structured, long-term relationships with individuals and community groups. Another important facet was the way in which Young Vic shows were developed. Local school groups were invited into the theatre to watch, participate, and contribute to the rehearsal process. Thus the work with schools, young people, and local residents informed, and was informed by, the shows the theatre was making.

Over the years TPR evolved into Taking Part, keeping a dialogue between the community and the performances in the theatre at its core. Dedicated workshop projects are run by directors from the Young Vic Directors Program, alongside Taking Part project managers. Assistant directors from each show lead schools workshops after the students have visited the theatre. Parallel productions, using an abbreviated version of shows produced in the main house but with a different, younger creative team, take place twice a year with local young people. Local residents and community groups participate in workshops inspired by the professional productions. The Young Vic also stages large-scale shows with a non-professional community chorus alongside the professional cast, such as *Tobias and the Angel* in 2006 and *The Human Comedy* in 2010.

Emmas' particular influence has been in making sure that Taking Part is not separate from the rest of the work that

FIGURE 17 *Young Vic Theatre, Tobias and the Angel (2006).*
Photo: Keith Pattison.

happens at the Young Vic but is fully integrated with it. She
has insured that the starting points for all Taking Part projects
are the plays that the Young Vic produces. The Taking Part
projects, in their turn, introduce new participants to the
theatre, helping to augment the diversity and vibrancy of the
audience. As David Lan, the current artistic director, says,
the theatre's goal is 'making great plays for great audiences'.
Under Lan's leadership, the Young Vic is committed to
creating a deep relationship with its local audience, believing
that this is the best way in which a community is sustained by
and sustains a theatre.

* * *

The *Young Vic positions itself firmly in Lambeth and
Southwark through its engagement with those two boroughs
which makes it a very local community engagement. What do
those words, 'local' and 'community' mean to you?*

For me, it's coming at it from a different angle. When we started thinking about what we wanted to do, we took nothing for granted. We wanted to look at what makes the Young Vic special, what we do well. So what are we? We're a building. And where are we based? We're based in Lambeth and Southwark. What do we make? We make theatre. So it wasn't about making a community theatre or thinking about being local – it was just what we are and what we do. Because we're based in Lambeth and Southwark, it became about Lambeth and Southwark. We recognised that within the locale of the Young Vic it would be good to get to know your neighbours, to find out what they felt about this building in their neighbourhood. In those days there were just two auditoriums and a really small thin café-bar that, once the show had gone in, was absolutely empty. The Cut wasn't a place where people came socially because it had nothing to offer. The huge change in the last twenty years just on this street has been phenomenal.

We wanted to establish relationships with people, so the invitation we issued was simple: we're here, you're here, come and see what we are and what we do. This is what we think about the world, what do you think about the world? It was an exchange. If people said, Oh theatre's not for me, I don't like it, we'd say, what have you seen? What have you been to? Nothing? Well, come and make an informed decision then. If you don't like it, fine, but come and see it first. We were part of their community and they were part of our community.

It's clear that you love theatre. Why do you want other people to love theatre?

I think it's like anything that you're passionate about, if you like football you want other people to come and engage with it. But I think for me, theatre is about empathy: you can be transported, understand someone else's life, maybe be changed, touched or surprised by it. Theatre gathers people together, we hear people's stories.

Taking Part's work takes that a step further – why do you think it's important that people engage with the experience of making theatre?

We say, come to see theatre and if you are interested in it, find out a bit more about the skills that go into making it: it's fun and you might decide that this is a vocation. Without this access or opportunity, you wouldn't know that a lighting designer exists because when you come and see theatre you don't necessarily see how all the pieces fit together. I don't ever want to demystify theatre's magic *per se* but to be able to see the component parts helps you to talk about it, helps you understand what you've just seen. It gives you a new language.

Take *Match of the Day* – there's a football match and the commentators break it down into sections to analyse it. Why do people turn up on a wet Sunday morning to play football? They might not be brilliant at it, but it's the sheer fun of doing it. You know you'll never be as good as Joey Barton, but you love watching it and you like playing it, and there's no reason why those two things should be mutually exclusive. Why not give people this opportunity in theatre – of flexing those muscles, of doing what an actor does, doing what a director does? You don't have to want to be that professionally, but there's still a joy in having a chance to do it. This knowledge through participation doesn't stop you getting carried away by the performance but you do have a better sense of the skill set, the craft, the magic.

Within the Young Vic's Participation and Schools programmes with young people, there is the possibility that this engagement with theatre could lead to a potential career. That is perhaps not the case with the Two Boroughs participants. Is there a big difference in the offer the Young Vic makes between those strands?

I think it is different. Even to the young people I think half the time you're saying look, if you want to work in theatre, to

FIGURE 18 *Young Vic Theatre,* Tobias and the Angel *(2006).*
Photo: Keith Pattison.

be poverty stricken, make an informed decision! But actually
if you just wanted to do it as an amateur activity, great. It's
interesting that you can play an instrument and no one thinks
you necessarily want to go and join the Philharmonic, but as
soon as you get someone to act, they instantly think you expect
them to go and be in a film or on the telly. It's a ruination of
amateur art. But of course we are always encouraging and
supportive of anyone who does want to pursue theatre professionally. And there are lots of examples of people who have
decided to become actors or directors and have worked at the
Young Vic professionally. That's really exciting.

*Do you think the Young Vic has a responsibility to say to
Taking Part's participants, your stories are as interesting as the
stories we choose to put on the stage?*

Everyone's story is interesting. So yes, of course. But art is
a filter. A naturalistic modern rendition of a story about the
death of a parent and betrayal by another won't necessarily

be as rich as *Hamlet*. The distance might give us a better way to explore our own lives. I think we have a responsibility as humans to be interested in people's stories. The act of making theatre is an act of making sense of the world. But it's never ever saying that if you don't do those workshops you can't watch a show and understand it. It's never about saying, do the workshop on *Macbeth* because then you can come and see the show and understand it. It is saying, the act of doing this thing is, in itself, fun. We don't work with 'issues' in the way other participatory theatre does, we do deal in stories, because that is what is interesting and vital, rather than it being a responsibility. For some of the groups we work with, for example women who have experienced sex trafficking or substance misuse, the theatre workshops are an opportunity for them to see themselves as creative beings, to explore all that complexity in a safe environment and also for us to perceive them in a different way. They don't necessarily want to tackle their experiences head on. A more cursory route is safer, more liberating and revealing. You don't just want to be defined by your life experiences. Sometimes we understand our own lives through the reflected filter of someone else's. It might seem that theatre is helping us escape our lives when actually we are getting further inside them.

In the Young Vic Directors Programme the theatre has a well-established network of emerging directors who lead a lot of the work that the Taking Part department does. Was that a conscious decision to make sure that those directors engaged with making theatre in a community context?

I think it comes back to a philosophical standpoint which is to make sure every aspect of the theatre organically feeds into every other. Within Taking Part, you mainly start through Schools, we then get the young person's name and address and send them invitations to Participation. When they've been to Participation, we invite them to come with a parent to see a Christmas show. So then the child is inviting the parent to the theatre. We might then invite the parent to participate through Two Boroughs. So we're trying to create pathways into the theatre and to see how they can interlink. When we started thinking about the directors' programme it seemed natural that it should fit into the wider world of what we do. Taking Part is integrated and integral to the whole artistic vision of the theatre, as is the Young Vic Directors Programme. So it makes sense for those strands themselves to be interlinked.

How much impact then, do you think working with community participants has on a director's practice?

Everything you do has to be robust. You'll be questioned on things in a way you won't be necessarily with professional actors. It will hone and clarify what you think. It can validate what you're doing, but it can also severely test it. And it questions your worldview as well, which is great, because if you work in theatre you can end up in a very monocultural environment where everybody is liberal, we share similar reference points or life experiences. So you have to be on your toes, ready to absorb and learn and reflect and react. If you are in touch with different people it will inform who you are as a human being, which will inform who you are as an artist.

The Young Vic's audience is well known for being young or diverse. Do you think that has a tangible effect on the theatre or on the theatrical moment?

You try and get on stage and in the audience something of a reflection of who's out there in the world because then you're not all responding to something in the same way, you're seeing different aspects of it and that can absolutely influence the live event. At the Young Vic the spaces were designed to be flexible, but also to be open, to be responsive: the audience can't ignore the actors and the actors can't ignore the audience because of the physical openness of the space, so you're joined altogether in experiencing something.

All theatre in some ways is community theatre because

every auditorium is made up of a community. It's a changeable community, but it's still a community. But I think you should never second guess your audience. You want to tell the story, in the way you want to tell it. But you have to know that the people are going to react to what they are seeing – sometimes literally. Especially audiences who are liberated from the constraints of 'nice theatre etiquette', as ours is. As with all relationships, it's a sense of connection. We wanted to make the Young Vic as open as possible to people to come here and have a brilliant time seeing brilliant theatre. When a teacher remarked that the young, mainly black, students walked through the doors saying 'This is my theatre' we felt we'd achieved something. We have a serious relationship with each of our audiences: there's a real exchange of ideas, belief, care and respect.

I get so tired of people saying that if you give free tickets away no one values them. They have the value that you – and other people – place upon them. If you treat things with respect and care and *give* them with a sense of respect and care, in this case the tickets, then they will be received in that way. It doesn't matter whether or not something has a price tag attached to it. Good theatre is an act of giving and an act of receiving all at the same time. There are very few things that do that. Art is a gift.

So the Young Vic is always offering an invitation, a welcome. There's no stage door here and it's significant that everyone comes through that same front door. A lot of people say that the building feels like 'home'.[1] How do you maintain that invitation, that homeliness?

---

[1]Zoe Svendsen carried out a series of on-camera interviews asking people who use the Young Vic about their relationship to it. The film, 'Young Vic in Conversation,' was commissioned as part of a retrospective of Haworth Tompkins, who re-designed the Young Vic, to be shown at the Venice Biennale in 2012. One of the major themes that emerges in the film is people's sense of belonging and ownership of the Young Vic – a lot of people said that they felt like it was home.

There are two things which enable this; in general the physical building (and specifically the main auditorium) and our approach to people. When we were planning the rebuild – which Howarth Tompkins and David Lan did brilliantly – we didn't want to change what we had, we wanted to make it better and just a tad bigger. The public spaces were really important. The people running the bar, The Cut Bar, had to really embrace what we were doing as a building: some people will never buy a drink when they visit, others might drop in for workshop sessions in the day or come around in the evening, gathering in the space but not using the bar. And you have to try to keep prices as low as you can or give opportunities for eating and drinking in a way that won't put people off coming to this theatre.

We also knew we wanted another studio space and we made a decision not to have a rehearsal room. We wanted the groups – whether they were from the Directors' Programme or Participation or Two Boroughs or the Schools and Colleges – to know that they were in a *theatre* space and that they were using the same spaces the professionals use.

When we started doing this, there were a lot of audience development programmes elsewhere that weren't fulfilling their promise. People asked us, how are you getting these results, couldn't you roll it out, make it bigger? But the Young Vic does everything through one-to-one relationships. Particularly vulnerable groups that we work with or schoolteachers who are under a lot of stress need to trust the person who represents the theatre to make their relationship with it as easy as possible. The reason people will come is because they trust the person making the offer. These personal relationships need a degree of focus: the more you extrapolate it, it stops having that kind of heartbeat, that kind of personal quality to it. We are who we are and what we are as a building and a theatre because it's personalised. We don't make a fancy leaflet with a great big print run. We get out there, talk to people and then they talk to other people. When they come to the theatre, we treat them with interest and care. It is like welcoming them into our home.

The Young Vic puts on community shows that have a mixture of a professional and non-professional cast. Why do you do these?

The community shows began because we started thinking, we've got these different strands – Schools, Participation, Two Boroughs – and we want everything to try to move towards some sense of being a culmination of all of them, of being holistic. It might be that you've come through a particular group, Afro-Caribbean elders for example, and done a project just with that group. And then we can say to those people, we've got this community show and you don't have to come with your group, you can come on your own, through Two Boroughs as an individual. That was very important for some of the vulnerable groups we were working with because suddenly they weren't the ex-sex worker, they weren't the person with the mental health problem, they were just a person who was there in the community show. It was also about reflecting the diversity of Lambeth and Southwark. So there was a barrister mixed in with a stay-at-home mum, with someone who worked for the local authority, with a young homeless person who lived in a hostel: this amazing mix. We are saying to all of these people, we're giving you our main stage, you're going to do a show and our relationships with you are so important that we're investing £250,000 in making this show. And we're going to stick professionals in there as well because what's better than your amateur Sunday football match than if Ryan Giggs turns up and you all play together? You're going to learn more and you're going to up your game. And the professional actors think they better up their game as well. It just creates a really amazing experience for everybody and they became shows that weren't 'community shows', they were just shows that had members of the community involved in them.

The first thing we did when we re-opened the building in 2006 was *Tobias and the Angel*, a community opera by Jonathan Dove, written for children's choruses, an adult chorus

FIGURE 19 *Young Vic Theatre*, Human Comedy *(2010)*. *Photo: Keith Pattison.*

and professional singers with a professional band. It was just phenomenal to get all of those elements together. It felt like a way of bringing all of the strands together and celebrating them and really seriously recognising the commitment and excitement we had about those people who'd dedicated their time to us. The show said very clearly, this is who we are, and we are proud of it.

10

The artist in collaboration: Art-making and partnership in the work of Mark Storor and Anna Ledgard

Sue Mayo

Introduction

Individuals working in community contexts call themselves many things other than artists: facilitators, theatre makers, theatre practitioners and animateurs, to name but a few. This variety reflects the diversity of the work, the range of roles and the sensitivities about them. Mark Storor always works collaboratively and is very specific about his identity as an artist: 'I would always say that I am an artist and that holds me in the work all the time. I only want to function as an artist when I'm in a room with people and I think they're functioning as artists too.'[1] For Storor, art is being made throughout all phases of a project. He does not use the polemic vocabulary of process and product, the way of describing the difference between the work that is exploratory and preparatory, and what it leads to: an outcome that has been edited, rehearsed and presented, in live or recorded ways. As a practitioner this interests me. I am aware that an over-delineation of spheres of activity can lead to a neglect of the quality of work going on during the 'process' and, equally, a neglect of the sense of ongoing development once it is in performance.

Crucial to Storor's practice are a carefully negotiated set of partnerships. He works closely with a team of artist collaborators, producers, organisations and participants in his projects. A photograph of Storor at work shows him kneeling on all fours in a workshop space, his hands on large pieces of blank paper, looking up with curiosity at the tulip covered feet of participant/performers. He is right in the middle of it all. This place of deep engagement is made possible by a robust network of relationships.

An examination of the work that Storor undertakes with educationalist and producer Anna Ledgard opens up arts practice that allows art and social engagement to flourish together. In this chapter I want to understand more explicitly the nature of art-making that allows and invites a quality of work that Helen Nicholson has called 'immediate, sensory and deeply personal'. This quality is the antithesis of the 'pedagogical clumsiness' that she writes about seeing in too much work with educational intentions.[2] I will explore the ways in which partnership underpins what Storor and Ledgard do and the nature of the creative work for which these partnerships provide the structure. This exploration

---

[1] Mark Storor, interview with Sue Mayo, 2011.
[2] Helen Nicholson, *At Last – Educational Theatre that Can be Called Art*, post on www.guardian.co.uk/theatreblog (accessed 18 April 2012), writing about a performance of *Boychild*.

is situated in the context of concerns and reflection about the role of the artist in relation to the different communities with whom they might collaborate. There is always the risk (and there are examples to evidence this risk) that an artist might *use* a participating group – as a commodity, as a provider of stories, as fuel, as free performers – to fulfil an artistic vision that remains entirely in the control of the artist: this is not collaboration. Dialogue, translation, debate, barter, adjustment, insistence and appreciation are among the acts of engagement required of an artist working with communities.

In *One Place After Another: Site Specific Art and Locational Identity*, Miwon Kwon explores evolving practices of site specific work in visual art, particularly the relationships between artists and communities that emerge in these practices. She raises many of the issues that are also present for theatre artists working in collaboration with communities and groups formed for the purpose of a project. Kwon highlights the artist who comes in as 'expert/exotic visitor';[3] the project where 'the siting of art in 'real' places can also be a means to extract the social and historical dimensions of these places in order to ... serve the thematic drive of an artist';[4] and tensions over who has the right to create representations of a community.[5] She also highlights practice where the art is informed by an attention to the building of relationships in order to allow dialogue and flexibility, for example John Ahearn's long relationship with a community, where he developed 'a very specific economy of intimate exchange'.[6] It is because it is possible to achieve this 'intimate exchange' between an artist and the participants that collaborative work can be so rich and so resonant.

---

[3]Miwon Kwon, *One Place After Another, Site Specific Art and Locational Identity* (Cambridge, MA: The MIT Press, 2004), p. 52.
[4]Ibid., p. 53.
[5]Ibid., pp. 88–92.
[6]Ibid., p. 88.

To assist me in this critical reflection I will also consider the work of two artists from other fields who have published reflections on their practice: the US-based choreographer and dancer Liz Lerman and Swiss potter Daniel de Montmollin, who lives in France. Both Lerman and de Montmollin identify as artists *and* collaborators. The sense of art at the heart of the practice that they share influences their navigation of partnership, engagement and aesthetics and this resonates with Storor and Ledgard's work. My focus will be the *how* of what is done, more than the *what*, in order to try to articulate something of the role, task, vision and territory that Storor's and Ledgard's work illuminates. My case study is *For the Best*, which was presented at the Unicorn Theatre, London (2009) and the Gostin's Building in partnership with the Unity Theatre, Liverpool (2010). The evaluations of both productions by Suzanne Steele and Aylwyn Walsh and conversations with Storor and Ledgard have been invaluable in opening up the workings of *For the Best* in both locations.

Mark Storor and Anna Ledgard

Storor and Ledgard first met on *Grown-Up School,* a piece conceived and created by Bobby Baker, commissioned by LIFT in 1999. At that time Ledgard was the Director of the LIFT Teacher Forum and Storor had been engaged to run the exploratory work with children. Both had roots in education: Mark trained as a drama teacher and Anna is an arts educationalist and producer who, with Tony Fegan, then Director of LIFT Learning, developed the Teacher Artist Partnership Programme (TAPP), as well as other strands of work. Anna's roots in teaching were:

> where I learnt the importance of devising entry points for all students into the learning process and where I practiced and understood the value of drama in engaging and giving

access to content of all kinds ... When I met Mark I met an artist who seemed to be working with individuals absolutely through the kinds of very motivating, inclusive ... engaging processes which really listened to the contributors. I could see in his practice as inclusive a practice as I had ever seen an artist working through.[7]

Since *Grown-Up School* Storor and Ledgard have continued to collaborate, their work characterised by long periods of research and development with their partners – the organisations, groups and communities with whom they work. It is marked by innovative and bold aesthetic, site specificity and an ongoing responsiveness to the participants' stories and ideas.

While the work that they have developed and undertaken together, and work that Storor undertakes with other partners (including ArtAngel, Artsadmin and the Roundhouse), attracts significant critical acclaim, it is the way in which Storor and Ledgard work together and the way in which they work with participants, artists and partner organisations that is at the heart of this investigation of collaboration.

Storor and Ledgard's first independent collaboration was *Visiting Time* (2004). Ledgard was interested in looking at how it might be possible to work with an artist on a public engagement project in a hospital during the working day. This project was followed by *Boychild* (2007), a study of masculinity and what it is to be male. Over a hundred men and boys participated in the making of this, culminating in a performance on Father's Day. Both pieces explored the world of science but particularly as it impacts most closely on human lives and experiences. Several themes emerged in these projects that continue to inform and thread through the work they do together.

The first is partnership and the mutual understanding that this demands. In *Visiting Time*, for example, the part of the

---

[7] Anna Ledgard, interview with Sue Mayo, 2011.

work that was with a school was with a mainstream curriculum group, 'completely as part of the fabric in partnership with the teachers'.[8] It was devised with help from hospital staff, a geneticist, and a patient at the hospital with cystic fibrosis. The support of staff at the hospital and the school was absolutely crucial and the team of Ledgard and Storor supplied both the vision and the structure that enabled that support: 'We understand that to be artists in a hospital or a school or whatever community it may be, we have to understand their language and their frames of reference and the way they're organised, and we absolutely respect that.'[9]

The second is that of the different skills that they each bring. Their partnership is 'values-led' and Ledgard works to create the structures and conditions in which the creative work can take place: what Storor describes as 'the scaffolding'. Both roles are crucial, and Storor and Ledgard clearly acknowledge the need to understand each other's roles, to cross over, while maintaining distinct responsibilities. In order to achieve, for example, a workshop led in the school by the young man with cystic fibrosis, and performance in the hospital while it was operational, both Ledgard and Storor needed to be able to articulate and demonstrate the practical and the aesthetic value, to one another, and then to the partners who were crucial to enabling these things to happen:

> At the beginning of the process Anna and I work very closely, [partners] meet both of us, we have our own roles, we talk about different things, but actually I'd say we've a code of practice which is about being professional, and saying we are driving this together.[10]

---

[8] Ibid.

[9] Ibid.

[10] Aylwyn Walsh, *For the Best: Liverpool Evaluation Report* 2010 http:// annaledgard.com/wp-content/uploads/report_final_online_SP.pdf (accessed 8 December 2012).

The third is the sense that the same ambition is present in the whole span of the project; that art is being made throughout, and the performance is a marked moment in time, but one where the art is still growing and developing. In the booklet that accompanied their second show together, *Boychild*, Storor describes the performance as 'like a scan ... a mere glimpse of the whole'.[11] For *Boychild* Storor had worked with men and boys in schools and working men's clubs, in a young offenders' institution and with fathers-to-be. From the start Storor introduced materials and objects that could disrupt and awaken; babygros, bread dough, hospital pyjamas. Throughout the exploration of what it is to be male, the practice offered by Storor offered the possibility to engage in a playful way with the distilling of responses into images and metaphors. New choices were still being made at the time of the performance, but for Storor this is simply another phase because 'there's a performative quality to the workshop every single time'.[12]

The fourth is the area of exploration. Ledgard describes their first two collaborations as 'experiments on the boundaries of theatre and science'.[13] Both *Visiting Time* and the subsequent show, *Boychild*, were collaborations between West Dorset General Hospitals NHS Trust and Education Departments in West Dorset, funded by the Arts Council and the Wellcome Trust. It is interesting that different nuances in the aims of the project can sit alongside one another, that of public engagement in science for the Wellcome Trust, alongside Storor's declaration, 'All I'm interested in what it is to be human and to be moved and to feel something

---

[11] *Boychild*, booklet to accompany show (2007).
[12] Mark Storor, interview with Sue Mayo, 2011.
[13] Anna Ledgard, *Visiting Time* and *Boychild*: *Site Specific Pedagogical Experiments on the Boundaries of Theatre and Science in Experiments on the Boundaries of Theatre and Science* (London: Wellcome Foundation, 2007), p. 111.

even if you don't know what it is.'[14] This comment reflects Storor's deep fascination with the human condition, one that he embarks on with others in a co-exploration. The aims come together in what Ledgard describes as 'communities of curiosity'.[15] While *Visiting Time* investigated the impact of genetic inheritance, and *Boychild* the experience of being male, both pieces began with and were led by the experiences of the participants: 'Once I'm working with people, ethically it has to be about what those people start with.'[16]

At the same time, Storor wants to take these moments and use them to trigger exploration. He told me a story about a moment during his time as a trainee drama teacher. He was working with a class in the auditorium of large secondary school engaged in a drama that was 'like a Western in Birmingham'.[17] There was a moment in the drama where a character incited the crowd to go and burn down a house nearby. The students, completely involved, ran for the door. Mark pursued them, blocked the door, and,

> I said something very dramatic like, 'If you do that we will never be able to meet again.' Whatever it was intrigued them and they froze ... And then we came back ... So I learned a way of doing things. But actually I was much more interested in everybody running out of the door and that ... in a way was the problem. Because I wanted to run out of the door and keep running, see what happened. Because actually there wasn't a house to burn down, but we were wanting something.[18]

This example is not, I believe, one that is principally about the difference between an artist and a teacher, although Storor did

---

[14] Ibid., p. 115.
[15] Ibid., p. 129.
[16] Ibid., p. 115.
[17] Mark Storor interview, 2011.
[18] Ibid.

not pursue a teaching career. The way in which this example points to his future work as a collaborative artist comes in his own examination of the example, 'I think part of the educative process is that it must lead you to places you don't know.'[19] The structure that Storor looks for in his work is one that allows him to follow the movement out of the door.

For the Best (2009)

For the Best explored the experience of living with renal disease, not just for those on dialysis but for their families. A collaboration with the Unicorn Theatre, London's purpose-built theatre for children, young people and families, Storor and Ledgard worked closely with children on dialysis in the Evelina Children's Hospital School. Once again, the Wellcome Trust provided the funding, with additional support coming from the Unicorn and the John Hedley Foundation.

For the Unicorn the project offered 'the opportunity to become involved in a model of participation which allowed space and flexibility for young people to give shape to their experience through theatre making and to be co-creators of the work'.[20] (Storor had run a two-day workshop with staff at the Unicorn to introduce his methodology before they agreed to the partnership.) In *Visiting Time* and *Boychild* the participants were the performers (with the exception of a group of young offenders in *Boychild* whose ideas and voices were present in the visual aspects of the piece as well as in Jules Maxwell's soundtrack). In *For The Best* this would not be possible. Many of the children had very challenging health issues, and their medical care was paramount. Instead a group of actors took on and developed the stories and images that emerged from the period of exchange, interaction and creation

---

[19] Ibid.
[20] Susanna Steele, *For the Best: Evaluation* (Unicorn Theatre: London, 2008).

that took place in the Evelina Hospital School and in partner primary schools. There is no sense that the time that Storor and Ledgard spent with the children and their families was the preparation for the real thing, the show. It had value in and of itself. There is also no sense that the job of the process part of the project was only to unearth material, and the production part was only to make theatre out of this material. Speaking about his work on a recent project, *A Tender Subject* (Artangel 2011), Storor spoke about the three years of work that preceded the making of the public performance: 'There was a gift every day.'[21] Of course, the performance is often the only filter through which those outside the project can encounter the work. We, the audience, are not necessarily seeing all the 'best bits'. We have missed some amazing moments too, but they have informed all that we do see. The measurement of the value of the work is not deferred to the performance, it is continuous and present.

Storor worked as artist in residence in the Evelina Hospital School for two days a week for nine months. He worked individually with each child, supported by a team of artists with whom he had worked before, who were familiar with his approach: Jules Maxwell, Babis Alexiadis, Cathy Wren and Sofie Layton. Steele's evaluation speaks about 'deep immersion in making work that genuinely responded to participants' experiences and ideas'.[22] Storor listens out for images and metaphors, ready to provide materials that might give an idea or an experience form, a piece of thread, a jigsaw. He brings a lot of materials with him so that he can be ready to respond, but will also bring in objects or materials in order to follow up on the way in which someone expressed an idea or a feeling. He is also asking questions: *If you were an animal, what animal would you be? What colour is your weary feeling?* For Storor, these questions 'encourage dialogue, to convene a different

---

[21] Mark Storor interview.
[22] Steele, *For the Best Evaluation*, p. 15.

space to dream in, to consider other possibilities'. The answers may become tiny poems or texts, and again lead to images and metaphors. He introduces visual and other sensory activities that encourage reflection and a connection between outer and inner landscapes. Through these 'fragments of conversation, vague thoughts can crystallise in objects which take on new meanings in our creative hands, their creative hands'. Working with a group of mothers of patients, Storor picked up on their conversations about waiting around for hours in hospital and eating too many muffins. The next week he arrived with bags of muffins and together they created a 'muffin mother' figure, an image of feeding and being fed, of boredom and of home, which found its way into the final performance.

Working within the Evelina Hospital meant getting to know not only the children but also medical and teaching staff, families and timetables. Storor speaks of the mutual trust and understanding that enabled the project: 'The nurses trusted me to be able to move around the space doing these things. That's important, they didn't detain me because they knew I was doing it within the constraints that they were working in.'[23] The trust also depended on his willingness to be in the real life of the ward. One child with whom he worked was often sick, so he continued to work with her, but also helped to hold the bowl and clear it away when necessary. He told me about a child whose permacath – a temporary catheter – got a bit infected and came out. When he came into hospital, it was hard to get him onto the dialysis machine because he had pulled out his stitches.

He was just so miserable, and said, 'It's that stitch, that naughty stitch,' and I just happened to have a reel of cotton in my back pocket and I said, 'Hold that, right, hold that.' He was hooked up to this machine and he said, 'and the nightmare came and just pulled this naughty stitch', and

---

[23] Mark Storor interview.

we just did it – I went all around the ward connecting everybody up to it, and he told his naughty stitch idea. And what was happening was that he had been feverish in the night ... wrestling with life and death really, and that became the moment (in the show) when the nightmare creeps into the bed and pulls the boy out of it by this thread and that's his story.[24]

This example of Storor working with just what was in the room, even when it was fearful and the child was in an acute state, is one both of responsiveness – being ready with the thread to materialise the story – and an immense trust in the process. It also needs to be seen in the light of the length of the residency in the hospital, so that the knowledge that the artist is there before and after such a moment is crucial to maintain a sense of ethical involvement.

Out of Bounds

There is another particular example of Storor and Ledgard's responsiveness that illustrates the way in which a significant part of the project could flow from a dialogue with one person, and then be supported through the partnerships that had been made, but that were still being tended and were developing. One child needed dialysis six times a week. Although he was on the register at a West London primary school, he was unable to attend classes there. The school supplied a learning support assistant (LSA) to work with the student in Evelina Hospital School, and work came from school to him through her. Initially uncertain about participating in the project, the boy gradually grew in confidence and in his enjoyment of the creative activities he was invited into. He wanted to be known by and know his peers in school, and he and Storor began to

---

24 Ibid.

develop a set of 'challenges' for his classmates. Based on the idea of a difficult journey, and informed by the images and metaphors that the boy's own reflective writing expressed, the boy developed, with Storor and others in his team, activities that used participatory drama techniques. These became *Out of Bounds*, a series of six three-hour workshops. Storor and his team delivered these workshops in the school. The children didn't initially know who had sent them this game of challenge. When they discovered who it was, their sense of connection to and understanding of their unknown classmate in hospital grew enormously and it made a huge difference to the boy himself. Despite the gravity of his condition this child subsequently visited his school and later the Unicorn to see the performance. The delicacy and respect that had been part of the development of work with him led to courage and an ability to take risks. It also significantly impacted on his classmates' understanding of the realities of his life and their empathy for him. His predicament had opened up a rich stream of creative and educational activity. In order to be able to be this responsive, the scaffolding provided by Ledgard was crucial, as she details below.

> It is significant on so many levels. Yes, it can only happen as a result of planning in close dialogue with all partners so we know what their priorities are – and it certainly helps that we understand the structures of school curricular organisation etc. But it was pretty obvious that something like this could work as soon as Mark met and talked to the child in hospital – most sick children want to have normal relationships with their peers if they can, but often there is simply not the time and expertise to facilitate this within schools or within the routines of a chronically ill child in hospital. We can bring our understanding of how the processes of art can achieve this. We ensure in the structuring of our projects that there is the time for Mark to listen and build a meaningful response based on what the child wants to do – in this instance the tools of drama, a letter from a

secret correspondent, the metaphor of a journey of extreme hardship etc. were the best mechanism to build a context of genuine difficulty which could build empathy. Mark uses many different strategies – those of educational drama, applied theatre, performance art – he dislikes being categorised as anything but artist, always seeking ways to listen and transform or metaphorise the experience of those he is working with as truthfully as possible. I bring the participatory framing within the institutional partnerships that enables him to work like this.[25]

But *Out of Bounds* went beyond the communication of one child to his classmates. Two primary schools were to be involved in the performances at the Unicorn, the children acting as guides for the audience. For Storor and Ledgard, it was crucial that the children were also connected in to the project at a point at which they could reflect and respond. Ledgard also wanted to be sure that the schools could find a way to connect these workshops to their own curriculum priorities: 'Ledgard sees the planning meetings that took place at the start of *Out of Bounds* as critical because they enable what she refers to as a translation process to take place.'[26] Here we see the collaboration, the co-creation that occurred between Storor and the child on dialysis, the connection this was able to facilitate between the boy and his class, and the continuation of the exploration with a group who were to be crucial to the performances at the end of the project. In all these stages we can see each partner bringing their specific skills and allowing him or her to make more than the sum of the parts.

The transition to the preparation of the performances at the Unicorn involved both continuation and newness. The artistic team had been working alongside Storor in the hospital. A

[25] Anna Ledgard, e-mail to Sue Mayo, 25 January 2013.
[26] Steele, *For the Best Evaluation*, p. 38

FIGURE 20 *Out of Bounds, For the Best (2009). Artistic Director Mark Storor, producer Anna Ledgard in collaboration with Evelina Children's Hospital, Charles Dickens Primary School, Unicorn Theatre, Artsadmin. Photo: Andrew Whittuck.*

tiger mask made by designer Sofie Layton inspired by a child's poem was used in the *Out of Bounds* workshop and in the show. Voices gathered throughout the project appeared in the soundtrack created by Jules Maxwell. In terms of the actors, Storor and Ledgard were looking for performers who would inhabit and respond to the material, who would be prepared to enter the process of discovery themselves. The six weeks of preparation for the show was a time to absorb and inhabit all the material that had already been gathered, but also to respond to it, to affect it:

> [Mark] gave us information and ideas from the children in a very careful way that enabled us as performers to explore ideas fully, examine them, turn them upside down and combine them with our own life experience to form a creative response.[27]

While this sense of openness and responsiveness recurs in people's reflections on Storors' work this should not suggest vagueness when it comes to aesthetic choices. Storor is clear that he is after clear, sharp aesthetic choices, 'by sharpening the aesthetic and keeping it bare you honour the story because there is nothing extraneous'. In all the accounts I have read and conversations I have had, there is no sense of Storor arriving at a finished product a week before performance and then making no further changes. This challenges habitual ways of working: familiar systems and structures of theatre producing, marketing and technical schedules. The challenge is taken on by partners because of the relationships Storor and Ledgard have built and the understanding they have generated about the nature of their work.

---

[27] Actor Gary Bates in ibid., p. 47.

The performance

The performance took over the whole of the Unicorn Theatre. Guided by children from the two partner primary schools, the audience was led through corridors and scene docks, in and out of a lift, and finally into a huge space where we sat on the floor among the performers. Installations and moments of performance inhabited the whole space, and I know that there were moments that I responded to immediately and others that I unravelled only some time later. With no distance between audience and performers, this was a sensory and immediate experience. In one scene a nurse clambered around the height of the huge scene dock, shifting heavy red ropes, with considerable effort. As she hooked and unhooked them, a boy sat below in his dialysis chair, bored and exhausted. Later this boy wrestled for his life, with death pulling him one way and his mother and the doctor pulling him another way. We so wanted him to live, and on the day that I went, he did.

The two nine-year old boys who I took to the performance were intrigued by a character who had accompanied us throughout our journey through the extraordinary installations and performative moments that populated the Unicorn. He had lurked and lolloped alongside the audience, often slightly hidden, throughout our journey. This character, we later found out was listed in the programme as The Nightbear. During the performance the boys were both very clear about who he was. For one he was fear, for the other death. When we met with him after the show, Storor said they were both right, and wanted to hear more about what they had seen and experienced. The rhythm of responsiveness continued. The art-making and the engagement with the stories was ongoing. He and his whole company held an enormously rich internal archive of all that had gone before, but the performance did not indicate a process that was finished.

Following the success of the performance at the Unicorn, Storor and Ledgard were invited to take *For the Best* to Liverpool. This wasn't a straightforward transfer of a production. As

FIGURE 21 *The Nightbear,* For the Best, *Unicorn Theatre (2009). Artistic Director Mark Storor, producer Anna Ledgard in collaboration with Evelina Children's Hospital, Charles Dickens Primary School, Unicorn Theatre, Artsadmin. Photo: Andrew Whittuck.*

Storor remarks, 'We said, Well that would be very interesting but of course it won't be the same piece because we need six months working on the unit in the hospital ... and we'll make a show that is very much about the Liverpool experience.'[28] For Storor and Ledgard this was not about repeating, but about continuing the development of the piece through a new set of partnerships. While the reaction was positive this is a very unusual response in terms of a theatre project. The performance is often the summation, the end point, and practically speaking, it becomes a way of continuing to earn money: it can be repeated. Storor and Ledgard made it clear that going to Liverpool was the continuation of a live process. Once again, partnerships were built. This time the residency was with a group of adults in the Royal Liverpool University Hospital Renal Unit, over four months, and with a group of primary school children, using the *Out of Bounds* series of workshops created in London. Built around the core of the London production, *For the Best* in Liverpool was enriched with new stories, different frames, and continued to evolve. Working in an adult ward, with ninety sessions of dialysis going on daily, was challenging. Issues for adults were different too, and these new stories were allowed to permeate and influence the piece. I was struck by Storor's account of an adult who he worked with in Liverpool who was a singer. Jules Maxwell recorded several of his songs, and Storor asked if one of them could be sung by the character of the Father at the end of the show:

And he said, 'Well I want that played at my funeral.' And he was really excited that he would have a copy of the song, and then, on the last day of the show he came and sang live ... and there was the father figure and the actual man standing by him singing. He wanted to do it and it's very important that we honour this thing.[29]

---

[28] Anna Ledgard interview.
[29] Mark Storor interview.

Articulating the practice

I want to turn now to two other artists because here we can find different iterations of some of the key themes that help to distil and define what these are. It is also interesting to look at Ledgard's and Storor's work within a wider context and see how others are exploring similar territory and articulating their discoveries. It returns me too to the broader theme, and the desire to articulate what this work, of the artist in collaboration can be about.

Daniel de Montmollin is a potter, based in eastern France. A brother of the Communauté de Taizé, he is a self-taught craftsman and has an international reputation. He discovered ceramics when, as a young monk, he had to care for a group of refugee children during the Second World War and discovered the potential of playing with clay. His own practice grew and developed, but he has always continued to explore ways of working with people with clay and, now in his nineties, is writing about this work and training other potters in his methodologies. His description of the way in which the artist in collaboration works with people is that of accompaniment. *Clay Shared: Key Words for Accompanying Creativity* is a glossary of the key themes present in collaborative work with clay, put together by de Montmollin and a group of six fellow potters over three years of research. Here they define Accompanying, Attention and Confidence. While these are not headings I have heard Storor use, they have a clear connection to the way he and Ledgard work.

> To accompany is to put a person in a situation allowing the discovery of what can happen to that person in an encounter with clay. The one accompanying proposes a setting that will give confidence to the one accompanied, giving access to a form of personal knowledge and expression.[30]

---

[30] Daniel de Montmollin, *Clay Shared: Key Words for Accompanying Creativity*,

To be attentive is to be receptive to what is already there as also to what may occur. It is the opposite of indifference and absence.[31]

Confidence is built up on three levels:
Confidence in the qualities of the clay;
Confidence of the one accompanied, in the experience of the one accompanying, a feeling that one will be guided respectfully;
Confidence of the one accompanying in the creative potential of the one accompanied.[32]

Returning to the sense of unease that can exist about ownership, about the locus of creativity, it is helpful to consider these clear images of the artist as a person with particular skills, engaged alongside a person or people with particular skills, and discovering, in the joint work, the creative possibilities, both 'what is already there and what might occur'. The artist 'proposes a setting', a structure within which the freedom to play can exist. Storor talks about the importance of 'the frame' – 'hopefully the frame around it is strong enough to hold what can happen within moments'.[33] The frame is not just the aesthetic frame, but also the whole scaffold of partnerships that have been set up to enable the work to happen.

And 'the work' is the meeting place. Kwon identifies the way in which a community 'sees itself in "the work" not through an iconic or mimetic identification, but through a recognition of its own *labor* in the creation of or the becoming of "the work"'.[34]

---

trans. Anthony Teague (Vendin-le-Viel: Editions la Revue de la céramique et du verre, 2009), p. 78
[31] Ibid., p. 72
[32] Ibid., p. 77.
[33] Mark Storor interview.
[34] Kwon, *One Place After Another*, p. 96.

de Montmollin is also very clear that the meeting place of the artist and the participant is in the work, in the joint venture, and that 'l'artist prend conseil de ce qu'il fait' ('the artist takes advice from what he is making').[35] He sees clay as a particularly inviting site for creative work, retaining, as it always does, the fingerprints of the maker. This seems to me to articulate very clearly what Ledgard and Storor do too. They respond to, 'take advice', from the work as it is in progress, and the fingerprints of the makers are all over the work.

Technique and knowledge are important to de Montmollin. While there is a very playful quality to the activities he describes, a fluency with the language of the art form is also necessary in moving towards what he calls 'creations': 'Creations can be defined, not as a goal to be attained, but as localized witnesses.'[36] These moments of acknowledgement that something has been made, and that choice was involved, lead to a greater capacity to create, and a confidence in this capacity. In the workshops in *For the Best* a poem or an image emerge from a conversation and Storor responds with materials that begin to grow the moment into something bigger. These 'creations' have a value in their own right, whether or not they arrive in the performance: 'Creativity comes first, technique is at its service, enriching and liberating it.'[37] The artist offers a way in to the exploration, through a game, an exercise, an invitation, and then accompanies, challenges and supports the participants as they make their discoveries. For Storor, 'the length of the process is so important, because it is in that time spent together that they start to manipulate the language and the images themselves, to become artists'.[38]

Like Storor, de Montmollin is also clear that the creative experience is shared, 'the other person's creativity enriches

---

[35] Author's own journal, 30 February 2004.
[36] de Montmollin, *Clay Shared*, p. 53
[37] Ibid., p. 68.
[38] Mark Storor interview.

me and vice versa. There is no secret to be jealously guarded. What I give is transformed by the other and returned to me enriched.'[39]

Storor and Ledgard both told me the story of an audience member and friend saying to Storor after *Boychild*: 'It's all about you!' I hear in this an anxiety about the risk of the artist becoming the focus of attention in a collaboration. Storor did not refute this comment, but stated, 'Yes, it is all about me, and it is all about them. It is all about us.'[40] Storor disrupts the idea of a neutral artist; he engages in the content alongside the participants. I have worked with a practitioner who articulated a very clear divide between herself as an artist, and herself as a facilitator, Storor and Ledgard's work, and de Montmollin and Lerman's reflections suggest that the term artist can travel between practices.

Liz Lerman is a dancer and choreographer, whose company, Dance Exchange, established in 1976, is based in based in Maryland, although their work takes them across the USA. In 2011 Lerman published *Hiking the Horizontal: Field Notes from a Choreographer* as 'a personal history of ideas and actions that emerge from making dances'.[41] Lerman's work cannot be contained in separated professional/community boxes, and she charts her own development through work that she taught to community groups, professional performances that contained dances by community groups, and work made collaboratively with the community. Hiking the horizontal is a phrase that emerged from a gesture. She describes showing with her hands the challenging of hierarchy, suggested by a vertical line that has fine art at the top and community art at the bottom, or vice versa, according to your view, by making it a horizontal. The possibility of journeying between the two

---

[39] de Montmollin, *Clay Shared*, p. 8.
[40] Mark Storor interview.
[41] Liz Lerman, *Hiking the Horizontal: Field Notes from a Chorographer* (Middletown CT: Wesleyan University Press, 2011), p. xv.

poles looks very different this way around, and in her descriptions of a rich array of her own work, describes a process where she is carrying the gifts of her professional and her socially engaged work from one place to the other, enriching both. She describes taking ways of working with elders in a community setting to her own company of dancers:

> I quickly observed that dancers committed more fully to work they helped build, that they often had better ideas than I did, and that my own role changed if the process changed. It got more interesting.[42]

At the same time she understands clearly what the place of the artist is in this collaboration. She describes the artist as both following and leading, being constantly alert to the way in which the co-created work is shaping itself. In her readiness to accept the way the work may well adapt and change I am reminded of Storor's desire to follow the action out of the door:

> pushing forward, either with questions or with preconceived ideas, and waiting for the spark to occur are twin activities. This is an easily misunderstood aspect of artistic process. Taking someone else's lead does not mean I have no plan or have a completely empty space in my imagination. It is more like leaving enough space for several possibilities to unfold. Including the one or more that I already have in mind ... The preconceived ideas may have sparked the reason people are gathered. The waiting may suggest that something better or more urgent may supplant the original thinking.[43]

While Lerman identifies the same reciprocity as de Montmollin, she also articulates the need for the artist to be alert to what

---

[42] Ibid., p. 177.
[43] Ibid., p. 22.

she describes as 'the fragment of worth'. For both Lerman and Storor performativity is always present as a possibility; they are on the alert for the moments and the stories that may emerge as part of what gets shown to others. She describes hearing a group of women talking in a workshop for *The Shipyard Project* (1994), and experiencing a shift in her perception as she heard a particular phrase: 'I realised the value of my own role as an artist in a moment like that. I was there to hear the poetry in a throwaway line.'[44] Joe Winston reminds us of the concept of *Erlebnis*, 'the most powerful expression of *an* experience as distinctive from the continuous flow of *general* experience'.[45] The skill of recognising these moments, intuitive as well as highly developed through experience, is part of what the artist brings to the collaboration. It brings ideas and images through from the experimentation and the discovery to the audience through being shaped and sharpened. Storor had thread in his pocket when the 'naughty stitch' was mentioned, but he needed to get it out and make a choice about what to do with it, that would enter into a dialogue with the child's story and serve to make it grow into a telling image. Ledgard described Storor's process as 'fishing. No, waiting for a rich rise of fish and then he'll respond and work with it.'[46] Lerman's image is also about fish, about discerning the shape in the water.

> I think that choreography is, in part, finding the fish: giving audiences some clues into the movement they are witnessing and even feeling in their own muscles and bones. These clues and images have their own shimmery edges that let us see what the artist sees and or that gives us a moment of private reverie into our own experience ... Once I saw

---

[44] Ibid., p. 53.
[45] Joe Winston, *Beauty and Education* (London & New York: Routledge, 2011), p. 47.
[46] Anna Ledgard interview.

the fish, then I got their movement and their story and then my story.[47]

In Lerman's writing I feel a clear sense of what Storor also emphasises, that art making is taking place throughout a project:

> rehearsals are not pretending. They are 100% real and demand absolute commitment ... We can't get to the next step if we haven't all focused together with great integrity and full emotional and physical readiness.[48]

Within the collaboration there is openness but there is also rigour.

Conclusion

Drawing the threads of these artists' reflections through my exploration of Storor and Ledgard's work on *For the Best*, some very clear themes emerge. The artists articulate mutual benefit. For de Montmollin 'the work returns to me enriched'. For Lerman the artist leads *and* follows. Ledgard speaks about the way in which, 'Mark's ideas merge with others' ideas.'[49] Many artists use the term 'ownership' in relation to the participants, as an indicator that the artist is not the sole occupant of the creative authorship and that participants are really engaged. But ownership is a definition that has its limits. I have used it myself to describe a quality of deep engagement with creative work; a sense of having a stake in it and a belief that one has influenced and will influence the piece of work. But I wonder if the practical use of the term suggests, and

---

[47] Lerman, *Hiking the Horizontal*, p. 67.
[48] Ibid., p.182.
[49] Anna Ledgard interview.

possibly desires, that participants have a greater control over content, form and organisation of work than they actually do. If the duration of a project, the dates of performance and sometimes the agenda or theme have already been determined before participants enter the picture, can they really own it? A whole set of decisions is not theirs to take. These artists demonstrate that collaboration is a term that better expresses the idea that the exploration, the discussion and the work created by *all* those involved are necessary and recognised. It is in the joining of forces, and in recognising the specific skills, interests and expertise that each person brings, that the work is able to happen.

At the same time, they remain artists in the space, not effacing their own practice in order to open up the creative space. Ledgard speaks about Storor's sense of being on the lookout all the time for images and ideas:

> he's alert. I would say he's at a heightened state of alertness. I know a bit what he's looking for but I could never second guess ... I'm able to help create the circumstances that things might come out in.

But Storor also is frank about needing to really want to be there himself: 'I'm only interested in doing things I'm interested in. There's no point otherwise. Because otherwise you're doing something *to* somebody.'[50] Lerman is aware of having an ear and an eye for moments that she can respond to and build on; she knows why she is there.

Art-making is going on throughout, and the performance is not the only indicator of the quality of the work. For de Montmollin the small signposts of 'creations' mark the constant bringing into consciousness of the invisible, and the participants are 'creators, not just creative'.[51] Ledgard remembers 'many

---

[50] Mark Storor interview.
[51] de Montmollin interview with author, 6 May 2012.

many completely extraordinary unforgettable moments within the hospital', including a moment when all the staff and children had to sing to tame a tiger that had appeared on the ward:

> Everybody rose to it, the consultants were singing *Waltzing Matilda*. It's a playful moment, but also a deeply serious moment because for that moment the children were absolutely on top of the game in the ward, and all the expert/child things were reversed in a way. That's what the artistic metaphor can do. It can change the expected way of doing things and that's what it did.[52]

Because of this, the process/product distinction dissolves:

> 'You're rehearsing all the time because there's a performative quality to the workshop every single time. But what you have to do is break down the performance that people do every time they come in, until you are a Company that share a language, which is richer and better than the mask you perform when you first come in.'[53]

Change happens through the work. Not just through the creative work with participants but through the structures that enable the work to happen. All of the negotiations with partners involve the building of trust, yet often trouble familiar patterns. Where the disruption and transgression reveal new pathways, there can be an increased confidence for future work. Ledgard describes work that has developed since *For the Best*:

> What I notice happens is that once institutions have worked with us this tends to build their confidence to invite us back and to define the terms of engagement themselves in a more active way with us. Evidence for this is provided at Evelina

---

[52] Anna Ledgard interview.
[53] Mark Storor interview.

where Sofie [Layton] and I are now working again, funded by the Guy's and St Thomas's Charity this time, with a mandate to involve staff and play therapists more fully in our process and thus to leave a legacy of skills within the institution. Sofie would say that working there is made very easy because the involvement of staff in *For the Best* means that there is an understanding and respect for the role that the art can play.

Storor returns to the central relationship, the artist with his co-artists – the participants:

the truth is we do intervene in people's lives. But you can intervene responsibly and it can be ok, so it's transformative in the time that you're doing it, [but] actually you don't know what will happen afterwards. I would say everything I do is political. But it's political in a very small way. You can say, there's another way of thinking about things or another way of looking at things, and I think that's political. Of course there are rules, of course there are ethics, however ultimately we are human beings and a very simple dialogue between one human being and another is rich beyond belief.[54]

Here art at the heart of the practice invites, unlocks and provides a language for this essential building block of existence. For the collaborative artist the collaboration begins with the 'dialogue between one human being and another' and needs to be replicated in the co-labour of carefully negotiated and dialogic partnerships between artists, with the participants as artists, with schools, hospitals, theatres and public.

---

[54] Mark Storor interview.

11

Tony Fegan

Interview and introduction by Caoimhe McAvinchey

Tony Fegan is a theatre director, arts learning practitioner and community arts activist. He has been the head of drama in an inner city London secondary school, director of Battersea Arts Centre (1985–9) and Director of Learning for London International Festival of Theatre (1993–2007). During his time at LIFT, Tony pioneered an integrated approach to learning which informed the organisation's programming, particularly its thinking about international and intercultural approaches to participatory arts work with children and young people from diverse social and cultural backgrounds across London. This work was characterised by long term, negotiated collaborations which were both politically and aesthetically ambitious. *Factory of Dreams* (1986), a collaboration between 120 13-year-old students from Stockwell Park School and artists led by the pyrotechnician Chistophe Berthonneau, culminated in a site-specific promenade of fire sculptures whilst simultaneously connecting to a number of curricular concerns. Project Phakama, an exchange between arts educators in

London and South Africa in 1996, evolved into a London-based youth arts organisation and global network of arts activists whose work shares a commitment to an emancipatory pedagogy. The legacy of this leadership has ripples in the work of individual artists and organisations from Argentina to Australia.

In August 2007 Tony Fegan became director of Tallaght Community Arts in Ireland.

* * *

Currently you are the Artistic Director for Tallaght Community Arts in Dublin – it's a name that boldly declares its commitment to a place and its people. How is this manifested in the work that you do?

Tallaght is a set of suburban communities, the overspill of Dublin's inner city out to greenfield sites from the late 1970s. It now houses 80,000 people, has one of the youngest populations in the Republic of Ireland and is very culturally and socially diverse. But when these people were first decanted to Tallaght there were no services: no schools, hospitals, doctors – nothing. So there was a very long period of time when people felt a real betrayal, anxiety and a bereftness of the inner-city sense of community, however difficult that was in terms of social and economic conditions. However, over the last forty years, Tallaght has been designated in popular imagination as a place of agitation, controversy and often been demonised. There's been tension between the traveller communities and the settled community. Drugs are a big concern. There's an awful reality show called *Tallafornia* and this epitomises how Tallaght has become shorthand for a perceived dysfunctionality from the middle class who fear them.

The organisation I took over in 2007 was called Tallaght Community Arts Centre (TCAC). But as we were on our way to becoming a tenant in a new county arts centre I said,

Let's take the 'centre' out of our name, and that was quite liberating. It let us think of ourselves as an enabling and facilitating organisation. Tallaght Community Arts is doing something very different now. It is working with professional artists who are very good facilitators and enablers of others. These artists are capacity builders, working very actively with the variety of communities locally; communities of geography, communities of specific economic, social and cultural backgrounds and, the one that I'm much more interested in, communities of interest – people who come together because they're interested in something irrespective of their backgrounds or locations.

TCA has had to work to reposition itself both within and beyond Tallaght. We are part of South Dublin County, a new county with incredibly old communities and villages like Lucan, Clondalkin and Rathfarnham, some of which are socially and economically very different from Tallaght. There's a lot of old territorialism. Whole areas of the county are bisected by big main roads that, literally, separate people. Across the country, there's no real public transport infrastructure so most people function by car. In Tallaght, we have a shopping centre which people drive into, do their shopping and then leave. We don't have high streets, so there's not much hanging about. We have a cultural quarter, built by the local authority, that consists of the county council offices, the county Library, the new county arts centre, RUA RED, and the Civic Theatre. There's a lot of plaza, car parking and empty buildings some of which are now in NAMA.[1] Over the last four years, with both the country wide financial crises and organisational financial challenges, my job has been to reposition TCA as an arts development organisation.

---

[1] The National Asset Management Agency (NAMA) is an initiative of the Irish government to tackle the country's crippling financial crises. NAMA operates as a 'bad bank', acquiring property development loans from Irish banks in return for government bonds.

I work in Tallaght in the same way that I worked when I was Director of Learning at the London International Festival of Theatre (LIFT): I asked, What are the interests that people have? What are the things we, as an arts organisation, can do? What use can we, as arts practitioners, be working in some sort of partnership with the people of Tallaght and the wider county?

We are connected with exceptional artists who have the capacity to work with people, inspire them and to bring them a set of skills or perspectives on the world around them. If I describe a couple of things that TCA has done it will help explain the politics of the practice.

There are a number of social and economic regeneration agencies in the area – Dodder Valley Partnership and Clondalkin Partnership – working at grassroots level with a lot of communities with social, economic and educational difficulties. Until recently few young people went to third level education and some of their parents may not have finished second-level education.

I got the organisation involved in something called ACT – Active Citizenship Together – which is a cross-county initiative by the South Dublin County Partnership (a social and economic regeneration agency) which brings in a whole range of agencies and community groups which operate in between the cracks, so to speak, including the Carers' Association, two traveller development groups and a drugs taskforce. The core purpose of ACT is getting people out to vote, to be active citizens in their communities and to consider what their vote means locally. At the time there was a lot of conversation about getting people's voices heard by their politicians – some listen more than others and some don't listen at all. So how do you get them to listen? How do you get heard?

Our response to this situation was *Box Stories*. We had 100 beautiful, big wooden boxes made and, through the ACT network, contacted about 120 different organisations and said to them, We can send you a box and three questions: Who are we? What are we? What would we like to say about ourselves? We offered to run some workshops to help groups think about what they could do with a box. The only conditions were no logos, no food in the boxes, and if you want to put a recordable device in it you've got to take responsibility for having enough batteries or recharging it. So, for four months, we did a lot of arts surgeries and saw lots of people whenever it suited them – at eight o'clock in the night, at eight o'clock in the morning, at two o'clock in the afternoon on the first Tuesday of the month, whatever it needed to be.

Ninety-three boxes came back from schools, youth groups, drugs rehabilitation people, elderly people, Tallaght Intercultural Drop-In Centre, the Carers' Association, the travellers' development groups etc. Some of them were exquisite in their artistic aesthetic. One box looked like it was embedded in a meteor with miniature paintings on the outside of it. A girls' school did a big pink fluffy one. A beautiful and very moving box was made by a traveller group. They tin-smithed it, decorated it and made a copper ladder with tiny little figures. This was the ladder of getting through life and there were people falling off it: it was about how many travellers just don't make it through life.

We exhibited the boxes in the County Library in Tallaght because it is the one place that has the biggest door – physically and metaphorically – locally. It doesn't feel so intimidating to go into. The mayor opened the exhibition and we had 2,000 people through the library on the first afternoon. People went 'Wow' because they could see each other through the boxes.

But the boxes had a life beyond the exhibition. Ten days before the launch, the ACT group organised a 'Meet the Politicians' night at a local hotel and thirty-five groups with their boxes came to the meeting and they talked about themselves through their boxes. It gave a moving and powerful focus to the evening.

There was also an event at the RDS,[2] *Claiming Our Future*, bringing together over 1,500 people to debate the idea of a new republic. We were invited to bring the boxes. Suddenly all these boxes went from Tallaght to a national event in the RDS in Dublin and lots of people from round the country saw them. That was really important: we felt that Tallaght was out in the world saying, this is not the place you think it is: there's something going on here. Pay attention to it.

We did another project, *Field of Dreams*, with a group of artists and local people about flags. We made very large, medium and small flags. The groups had to think about how they might express themselves through a flag, it wasn't just making bunting. We got one of the local social enterprise agencies to give us an empty unit as a flag factory, somebody lent us sewing machines and 500 people from 23 different groups worked on this including many people with disabilities and a group of young guys who had just come out of drug rehabilitation. We congregated in the cultural quarter adjacent to the council buildings and processed to the Shamrock Rovers Stadium, planted all the flags on the pitch, had our photograph taken and then everyone went off and had a party in the stadium. Many participants had never been in the stadium let alone on the sacred green sward. Both these projects were about the arts enabling the public manifestation of the dreams and aspirations of people and communities who often go unseen – for them to be seen in a celebratory way.

The reach of the projects, both in terms of who is included within them and who the audience is for them, is ambitious. TCA is, organisationally, you and another person working part-time with a team of freelance artists. How have you developed the capacity of the organisation to be able to do this work?

---

[2]The RDS is a Dublin venue named after the Royal Dublin Society, a philanthropic society committed to the economic and cultural development of Ireland.

We have been making lots and lots of connections with people locally and now they recognise us as people they can go to to have a conversation about making something happen. We've also been developing a network of artists which has evolved in different ways. We are committed to working with people with disabilities, who are some of the most marginalised in our communities. We run a studio where individual adults with disabilities come and paint or make with support of artist mentors. The studio is a social space in an arts building where these artists can come and legitimately be there developing their own practice.

I'm currently developing with Cindy Cummings, an American choreographer, a two-year project with a working title *House*. Essentially, it's looking at the making of Tallaght over the last forty years. We are hoping to get an empty house in Tallaght – which is highly political, because lots of people don't have houses – to use as a social space that gathers people and their stories of this place together. We'll invite people to bring things – their old 8mm or 16mm film from the early days of Tallaght, cassette compilation tapes made for street parties, old photographs, whatever they've got – and share it with each other and a wider audience. We may eventually build the quintessential Tallaght house in a gallery for it to become a repository for all of this stuff, mediated by the artists. If you turn on the telly you might see some old movie footage, if you open a book you might see some stories that people have written about what they remember as kids there. But it's not a reminiscence piece. On the walls of the gallery people may see the original archive materials and we'll have a series of live events.

Ultimately, TCA is working with the communities of people who live here to say to the wider world, Tallaght is a very interesting place to be, something is happening out here that's not happening in central metropolitan Dublin. In a way, we are a service organisation to the local community.

This is a very unusual proposition. In the USA, there is a term 'theatre in the service of …' that theatre work that is commissioned and has very clearly prescribed goals. Yet, this offer of service by TCA is responsive and responsible to the community, working in partnership with it towards co-defined development aims rather than something commissioned by an external body and done to or on a community. Rather than being beholden to funders and their agendas you are co-defining an agenda with the community.

I see TCA ultimately as an enabling service, inspiring a capacity building through the arts. Another recent piece of work gets us deeper into the methodology and the aesthetic of this idea of service.

Some of the groups that worked on the flags project went to the local council chamber, to see how the council actually works. One of the community groups had a very legitimate issue that's been going on for three years that they wanted to discuss with the councillors. However, they didn't present themselves very well and it caused consternation.

I realised then that one of the biggest things TCA might do is to work with local groups, representing particular communities of interest, to talk about what it is they want to be saying to people and how to organise it. So, what are the statistics around the issue, who have you written to, who have you spoken to, what are the human personal stories that you need to tell to make the issue clear? Again, working in partnership with ACT, we developed the project *What Matters?*

Two theatre artists worked with four groups with very different concerns. One was a men's group trying to address a range of issues, including the lack of male role models for young teenage boys and the high incidence of suicide amongst teenage boys, which is high in Ireland generally and certainly in some of our localities. There was a group of feminists, women in their late fifties and sixties, who went out and got an education when their kids had grown up. There was an intercultural group concerned that there are no official translation services in Ireland for people from different cultural linguistic backgrounds. A traveller group wanted to talk about how the travellers' support teachers had been taken out of the schools because of the cuts. Over eight weeks we worked with the four groups to support them organise themselves as a campaigning group working on ten minute performance presentations. Over 150 people turn up to see them and there were standing ovations after every presentation. The men did Hamlet's soliloquy, 'To be or not to be', whilst telling one man's personal story about facing suicide whilst another gave the statistics around suicide of young men. The intercultural group did a film with people talking in their own mother tongue and the problems about translation. Since then, there have been more groups, including a refugee group, that have expressed interest in going through this process.

These things are a service, but they also have an impact on the aesthetic arts. People can now see that artists are socially, politically and economically useful, that we have a central part in that social economy rather than running around on the periphery of it.

When you were Director of Learning at LIFT, ideas of learning through participation were central and integral to the ethos of the organisation. What informed this?

Before LIFT I was head of an expressive performing arts faculty at a community school in Kilburn, north London. We had everybody from eleven to nineteen and everybody from ninteen to ninety. When I was there, I did many things, including running a cultural politics course for adults returning to learning. Prior to that, I'd been at Battersea Arts Centre (BAC) for four years, and I had eight years at Holland Park School in Notting Hill Gate and was head of drama. It was one of the most socially and culturally diverse places that you could possibly work in. I had had a completely Euro-centric arts training and then I was in this school where we had fifty-seven different nationalities and a huge proportion of the first generation of black British kids.

Somebody once asked me, Why you do what you do? For me, it was always a sense of a social justice. I was a product of an immigrant family. I had a whole set of opportunities in England that I wouldn't have had in Ireland if we'd stayed there. It was a time when there was a commitment in the UK to free third-level education. I had a whole set of educational opportunities that my parents wouldn't have been able to afford for myself and my five siblings. I had a grant to go to college and I knew other people there who came from backgrounds where there were few expectations that college was something for them. We were of a generation that thought we were going to change the world.

When I went back to Ireland in 2007 I was profoundly shocked by the lack of a substantial arts curriculum in the schools there. I believe so many kids fail in Irish schools because if they can't do something that is conventionally academic there's no other place for them to fit in. The other shock was meeting people of my own age who hadn't had the opportunities that I'd had to just have an enjoyment and pleasure in the arts. Now, in their late fifties and sixties, they had a hunger to experience the arts, to participate in it. I believe that the arts should be a cultural entitlement in the same way that the National Health Service should be an entitlement. Of course there are responsibilities that come with that. But we should ensure that people can choose to have experiences of the arts and then choose not to, if they so wish. But many people don't even know that it's even there for them to make a choice. In a way, many people view the arts like they view going to a private consultant, they don't think it is for them or that they can afford it. That's a diminishment of ourselves as citizens in a country that we call a republic.

Given that Ireland, particularly during the years when the Celtic Tiger was roaring across the globe, promoted its artists and itself as a tax haven for artists and for film companies, why do you think this pride or sense of value doesn't infiltrate to thinking about the arts in formal education?

The arts are too troublesome. I believe that the Catholic Church and political parties in Ireland don't want a thoughtful population. For centuries, many of our citizens have been marginalised – and the arts were marginalised, ridiculed or even in the case of some artists excommunicated. What we are trying to do in Tallaght, in a small way, has to do with the business of cultural entitlement.

Recently we did a *Trashcatchers* carnival with a group of adults, older adults and children. There was a wife and husband, in their sixties, who took part in the project. He worked with an artist who showed him how to make these amazing headdresses out of wire. She got on her sewing machine and made Bottom's costume out of an old brown check blanket with a tail made with fishing wire. They had a great time. About a week later when I was talking to the community centre manager about evaluation she said that the project had had unintended outcomes, that this project had renewed that couple's marriage! The man and woman had spoken to her separately and told her that their kids had grown up and gone away and they had had nothing to talk about. Suddenly, with the project, they had been talking about what they'd been doing. So although they were doing things separately in the project they saw it as being part of a shared thing, as part of something together.

Participatory arts projects create new social space that has social moments when you have a mixture of people bumping into each other, saying hi to your neighbour, sharing something. In the end, that's the thing that's important, to be connected with other people. The work creates a community of interest. *That* I find interesting.

12

Paul Heritage

Interview and introduction by Caoimhe McAvinchey

Paul Heritage is Professor of Drama and Performance at Queen Mary, University of London and Artistic Director of People's Palace Projects (PPP), an applied performance research unit and arts organisation that develops and produces large scale international cultural projects driven by a social justice agenda. Much of this work takes place in Brazil or is in collaboration with Brazilian social and cultural partners. *Staging Human Rights* engaged over 20,000 prisoners and prison staff to promote dialogue about human dignity, rights and responsibilities in prisons across Brazil. *Favela to the World* (2006–12), a collaboration with Grupo Cultural AfroReggae saw a transition from working within the criminal justice system to the forging of partnerships with arts organisations created within communities fractured by gun and gang crime in Rio de Janeiro. *Cultural Warriors* (2009–12), an intercultural dialogue with Brazilian artists working with young people and organisatons in the UK, evolved from *Favela to the World* as a way of exchanging knowledge about the way in which art organisations support young people's development as community and cultural leaders. Recently, as part of London's Olympic and Paralympic celebrations – and in anticipation of Rio de Janeiro's stewardship of the 2016 Olympics and Paralympic Games – PPP produced *Rio Occupation London*, bringing 30 ground-breaking Rio artists to 'occupy' over thirty spaces across London during thirty days.

* * *

Throughout your career your work has been fuelled by an activist agenda. Why work in and through the arts?

Between 1984 and 1986 I was very engaged in community action around HIV and AIDS. It was urgent for very obvious reasons – it was about our own health, about saving each other, it was about life, love and death. Gay community activists in the United States ensured that the basic information about what people needed to do to protect themselves got to those who needed it. Here in the UK I learnt from queer cultural warriors that art had multiple functions – as activism, as fundraising, as political consciousness.

The first UK government AIDS awareness campaign was in 1986. It was a leaflet and then a television campaign. By then, over 200 gay men and haemophiliacs had already died. The state was not actively addressing HIV and AIDS but the community affected by the issues was already dealing with it. That was my switch-on moment.

I was lucky enough to experience that at twenty-four. By then I had started a professional career. I was an assistant director at the Royal Opera House, I'd been to Australia as an assistant director in opera and I was working at the University of Wales in Swansea as a lecturer. Both areas of my life – the professional arts side and the academic side – were bound together through my own personal activism with HIV and AIDS.

The first time I went into a prison was to do a safer sex workshop. The Act Up movement – the AIDS Coalition to Unleash Power – was very much about working with absolutely anybody who wanted practical information about safer sex. In the very early days, the original; high-risk' groups were the 'Four H's': homosexuals, haemophiliacs, heroin users and Haitians. That's how weird the time was. Governments were still trying to say AIDS was contained to certain identities, behaviours and populations. Prisoners – particularly male prisoners – were identified as being transitional groups. In the 1980s homosexuality was still illegal in public spaces and prison was a public space where it was illegal to have condoms, compromising any educational initiative. But at the same time, the authorities identified the potential cross-over risk back to the 'general' population.

As a result of going into prison to do the safer sex workshops, I developed an interest in prison theatre work, but the impetus for this work came from that initial switch-on moment: the belief that there was something to be done through art and activism.

Had you done any community-based theatre work before the safer sex workshops?

No. Far from it, as I was obsessed with opera. But somehow I didn't question whether or not I could do the work in prisons or elsewhere. My authenticity came from my own identity and my own experiences of being a gay man and the need and urgency to talk about safer sex and AIDS/HIV. When working with students later at universities in the UK and Brazil, I realise how privileged I was. Many students don't feel that authority or validity. They question themselves about what capacity or even what right they have to be doing an arts project in prison. The self-questioning is important but unless you can work from some position of strength of who you are, it's going to be very hard to be able to either respond to the invitation from somebody else to work with any group of people: to arrive with a sense of gift or dialogue. You have to have something of *who* you are and *where* you have come from in this work.

Perhaps this has led me to depend on being the outsider in so many circumstances where I have worked as an artist. However much I start any project looking to close the gaps between all of us who are participating, I always seem to keep a keen sense of myself as 'outsider'.

A prison is one of the hardest places to find human commonalities as it is built on division, separation and exclusion. But what you try to achieve is a sense of communality within a workshop or within a life experience, even if it is always at play with the sense of the person who comes in from outside. The two are always in dialogue. Thirty years on, I'm still playing on the axis of insider/outsider between Britain and Brazil. I seem to find it a productive, generative, creative mode.

After the ACT UP workshops, how did the prison theatre work evolve? Was there an invitation from the state or were you knocking on doors?

In Swansea in 1985 we first entered the so-called criminal justice system through working with young people on probation. Through that experience we were able to suggest to the authorities that theatre could be an effective health-education process for people in prison. Then in Manchester in 1989, I started working with Geese Theatre.[1] They stayed in my house while on tour to perform in HMP Strangeways and I asked if I could go in with them. That was a really important moment. I suggested to the prison that because I was based in Manchester I could carry on doing the theatre work when Geese moved on. From that experience, I went on to

---

[1]Since 1987 Geese Theatre Company has been developing drama-based interventions with offenders, young people who are at risk of offending and professionals who work with them within the criminal justice system. For more information see http://www.geese.co.uk (accessed 1st March 2013).

FIGURE 22 *Paul Heritage on stage with AfroReggae. Photo: Ellie Kurttz.*

establish the Theatre in Prisons and Probation Centre (TiPP) with James Thompson, who had recently graduated from the drama department at Manchester University.[2] Twenty years later, the TiPP Centre is still based there.

James and I were fascinated with the potential that drama offers to offence-focused programmes and approached Manchester Probation Service to suggest that we develop a project in partnership with them. To our great surprise, they commissioned us, and together with the designer, Jocelyn Meall, we created Blagg! in 1991. The commission was for

---

[2]The Theatre in Prisons and Probation Centre was set up in 1992 as part of the Drama Department at Manchester University developing theatre-based programmes in and in partnership with the Greater Manchester Prison service. It became an independent charity in 1996 and in 2000 changed its name to TiPP, reflecting the shift in its work beyond prison and probation to include work in community contexts with the long-term unemployed. TiPP continues to have strong connections with the Drama Department through teaching and research collaborations. See http://www.tipp.org.uk/tipp/ (accessed 1st March 2013).

£6,000 – the biggest grant I'd ever been awarded at the time – and even now I remember the excitement!

I was a drama student at Manchester when you and James had just set up the TiPP centre. I vividly remember the sense that what you were doing was maverick and vital, a surprise to both the prison system and to the university. It was certainly a provocation to students to think about theatre as activism. A number of your and James's students have since gone on to work in prison theatre specifically but also in arts and social justice more broadly.

I trace the deepest line of my work through the various universities where I have based my research and teaching – in Britain and Brazil – over thirty years. Structurally, philosophically and intellectually, the public university is the most dominant factor in everything. I worked from the simplistic belief that universities and prisons are public civic space. It framed my belief that it was completely natural and 'right' that students should be in the prison and that prisoners or probationers and prison staff should be in the university: through arts they could become common learning environments about life.

When I went to Brazil for the first time in 1991– to do a lecture series to accompany Cheek by Jowel's tour of *As You Like It* – I knocked on prison doors again to say I'd like to come and do workshops. Amazingly, I was invited by the prison complex in the Federal District of Brasilia to return and set up a project. The Federal University offered me a position as Visiting Professor and in 1992 I began to work between prison and university in Brasilia, just as I had in Swansea and Manchester. Later I did the same when I set up an AIDS-education project in four prisons close to the University of Campinas in the State of São Paulo and once more in Rio de Janeiro with UniRio.

The prisoners, guards, education monitors, directors and prison authorities offered me the opportunity to create work that I would never have imagined in the UK. The 'system' started to promote and multiply the projects. *Staging Human Rights* worked with over 20,000 prisoners and 1,000 prison staff in 12 states across Brazil between 2000 and 2006. It wasn't offence-focused – it wasn't about individual behaviour – it sought openly to changing institutions and institutional behaviour. The activist aesthetic was very important. It was key. We deliberately sought to distance ourselves from offence focused behavioural programmes and projects. Cognitive behavioural therapy or offence-focused work has an important contribution to make, but it's not what I wanted to do. In the Brazilian prison system there were other things that seemed more urgent.

As a citizen we give 'permission' to the state to take the liberty of somebody else away. I used that as my 'authority' to enter those spaces. It's our responsibility to be engaged in the consequences of our society: the difficulties, horrors and pains of the staff and the prisoners are just part of the hidden consequences of how we live.

When I set up the drama department here at Queen Mary, University of London in 1996, I was given the opportunity to create a parallel space to pursue my research interests. People's Palace Projects takes its name from a building that is now part of the QMUL campus but actually pre-dates the university. The People's Palace was opened by Queen Victoria in 1886 to provide educational and cultural activities for the people of east London. People's Palace Projects is both a practice-based arts research centre and one of Arts Council England's national portfolio organisations.

As British universities have become less public and the British prison system is increasingly privatised, the axis on which I built work has been replaced by new questions about the public civic roles for artists, activists and academics. These seem at present to be articulated best for me through a series of cultural dialogues, exchanges and encounters that focus on shared experiences between Britain and Brazil.

In Intense Dreams *you write about the absence of state support and how particular companies or practices in Brazil 'fill the void with an intensity that makes invidious any meaningful comparison with almost all British art space initiatives with a social dimension'.*[3] *You describe going into Carandiru – a now demolished prison in São Paulo which once housed up to 8,000 inmates and was notorious for the abuse within it – and your initial surprise at seeing a samba competition organised by the prisoners. They had a cultural framework in their own lives that was so established that it made this event unremarkable to them. With* Cultural Warriors *and* Points of Contact *you've developed exchanges and networks with artists and cultural practitioners coming from Brazil to the UK. Do you think the idea of a cultural framework in your everyday life exists in Britain? Is it possible?*

Those are crucial questions. We all know whenever and wherever we work in prison that our arts work probably has more impact in the lives of a prisoner or a guard than everyday arts experiences outside, because it's experienced in a vacuum. Participation in arts work in prison is often very powerful and there is a sense – when it's done well – that its absence will always be felt. What happens in the prison is very intense.

In poor, marginalised communities in Brazil – *favelas* and other peripheral communities – there has historically been another sort of vacuum. Brazil has been changing rapidly over the last decade, but for much of the last century, the state was inactive in these communities in terms of health provision, education, public security, housing, sanitation, etc. Residents became outsiders, even though they were often folded into the very physical and human geography of large cities. And so the artist and the cultural manifestations in those sites are fulfilling so much more than what the arts do in the UK.

In the last few years in the UK, artists and art organisations

---

[3]Paul Heritage, *Intense Dreams: Reflections on Brazilian Culture and Performance* (London: People's Palace Projects, 2009), p. 8.

have been so much more confident about articulating and claiming a transformative space for their work. Initiatives such as Creative Partnerships and companies such as Dance United forefront health, wellbeing, education and a wide range of social benefits in their public profiles. But it's not a very joined-up or coherent picture. In a *favela* in Rio or a prison in the Amazon, we can learn to see just a bit more clearly what the arts can offer. The Brazilian experience offers us a useful point of reflection.

Brazil is in transition. Increased resources and direct public involvement in marginal communities has radically transformed the relationship between the state and the individual. There is still absolute poverty on a terrifying, catastrophic scale, but quantifiable change has happened. As the Lula government of 2003–2008 set about seeking such basic material transformation on a mass scale, what role and what sort of priority would be given to arts and culture? Gilberto Gil (Brazilian Minister for Culture 2003–2008) and Célio Turino (Secretary of Cultural Citizenship 2004–2010) created the *Living Culture* programme as part of the government's economic and social development agenda. But unlike other government programmes, their focus was not on bringing new resources to impoverished communities, but on recognising and unleashing the existing resources. The investment they made was in creating new connectivities and flow for cultural activities that had ensured the survival of these communities. I wanted to know what we, in Britain, could learn from this programme. Could there be a genuine exchange between Brazilian and British policymakers and artists? The *Points of Contact* Brazil–UK exchange has been a really powerful way to understand what's so good in British culture and what lacking.[4] During their visits to the UK over the first three years

---

[4] *Point of Contact* (2012) was an exchange programme between artists, policy makers and funders from Brazil and the UK to create new dialogues about the possibilities of social and personal transformation through the arts.

FIGURE 23 *Artists and cultural policy makers from Brazil and the UK visit Complexo do Alemão during* Points of Contact *(March 2010). Photo: Ratão Diniz*

of the programme, Brazilians have identified that the UK has an incredibly vibrant, robust arts sector and arts institutions but they don't understand why we have no cultural policy.

What are you working on at the moment?

A UK cultural festival of young people's ideas – a collaboration between PPP, Battersea Arts Centre and Contact Theatre in Manchester inspired by the *Agência Redes para Juventude*, Youth Agency Network, in Rio de Janeiro.

Agência is run by an extraordinary figure, Marcus Faustini. When I first met him he said to me, 'My main aim in life is to get rid of people like you and me, because we are the problem. We are the people that get between young people and their own sense of agency.' He sets up incredible projects. As Special Adviser to the Secretary of State for Culture in Rio de Janeiro he created special funding programmes for hip-hop and internet cafes. As a cultural activist and leader he has set up a cinema programme for young people from peripheral communities, a poetry and philosophy school, a special project for street vendors and a *Dragons' Den*-style arts programme that creates 1,000 young cultural entrepreneurs every year. His main aim is to connect young people into the networks that will sustain them: to encourage them to recognise that culture is a territory that they can occupy and expand.

Who or what has been a significant influence in your commitment to art, activism and the possibility of community transformation?

In the UK? Noel Greig, Philip Osment and Gay Sweatshop changed my life. James Thompson was there beside me when it really mattered. In Brazil? Augusto Boal, of course. Julita Lemgruber and Silvia Ramos at the Centre for the Study of Public Security and Citizenship, Célio Turino and Gilberto Gil at the Ministry of Culture. AfroReggae, Nós do Morro ... it's impossible. But I want to say something about structures rather than individual artists or arts organisations. One thing Brazil is really good at is structures. I can remember how I first responded reading Augusto Boal in 1985. Boal was totally inspiring, an amazing speaker and great storyteller who articulated this incredible methodology. I've continued to be fascinated by other Brazilians who put creative methodologies into structures.

I remember the first time I directed anything in Brazil – whether it was Shakespeare or a prison theatre course – students and actors were really disappointed that I didn't declare my methodology or school of thought. There's something very British about that. But I remember when I worked with Lois Weaver and Peggy Shaw from Split Britches that they helped me see that it is okay to have an *approach* rather than a methodology – perhaps that is ultimately more liberating. And yes, and they are certainly two big influences!

PERMISSIONS

I am very grateful to the photographers, theatre makers and arts organisations that granted permission to reproduce the images in this book.

Lois Weaver for images of *The Long Table* and *The FeMUSEum*.

Magic Me, *Wisdom of All Ages* (performance). Photo: Julia Illmer, Magic Me.

Magic Me, *Wisdom of All Ages* (workshop). Photo: Magic Me.

Mojisola Adebayo and Mamela Nyamza in *I Stand Corrected* (2012). Photo: Taryn Burger.

The Lawnmowers Independent Theatre Company, *Boomba Down the Tyne* (Humsaugh Village Hall, Northumberland, 2012). Photo: Darren Eddon, Available Light Photography.

The Lawnmowers Independent Theatre Company, *Graeme's House* (2011). Photo: The Lawnmowers.

The Lawnmowers Independent Theatre Company, Ali Campbell and Paul King in a Lawnmowers' workshop. Photo: The Lawnmowers.

Bobby Baker, *Pull Yourself Together* (2000). Photo by Hugo Glendinning.

Bobby Baker, *First F.E.A.T.* (2008). Photo: Andrew Whittuck.

London Bubble, Poster for *The Blitz Show* (1972): Bubble Theatre Company's first production. London Bubble Archive.

London Bubble, *Blackbirds* (2011). Photo: Steve Hickey.

Young Vic Theatre, *Tobias and the Angel* (2006). Photo: Keith Pattison.

Young Vic Theatre, *Human Comedy* (2006). Photo: Keith Pattison.

Out of Bounds, For the Best (2009). Photo: Andrew Whittuck.

The Nightbear, *For the Best* (2009). Photo: Andrew Whittuck.

Paul Heritage and AfroReggae. Photo: Ellie Kurttz.

Paul Heritage, *Points of Contact* (2010). Photo: Ratão Diniz.

Rosemary Lee, *Common Dance* (2009). Photo: Simon Weir.